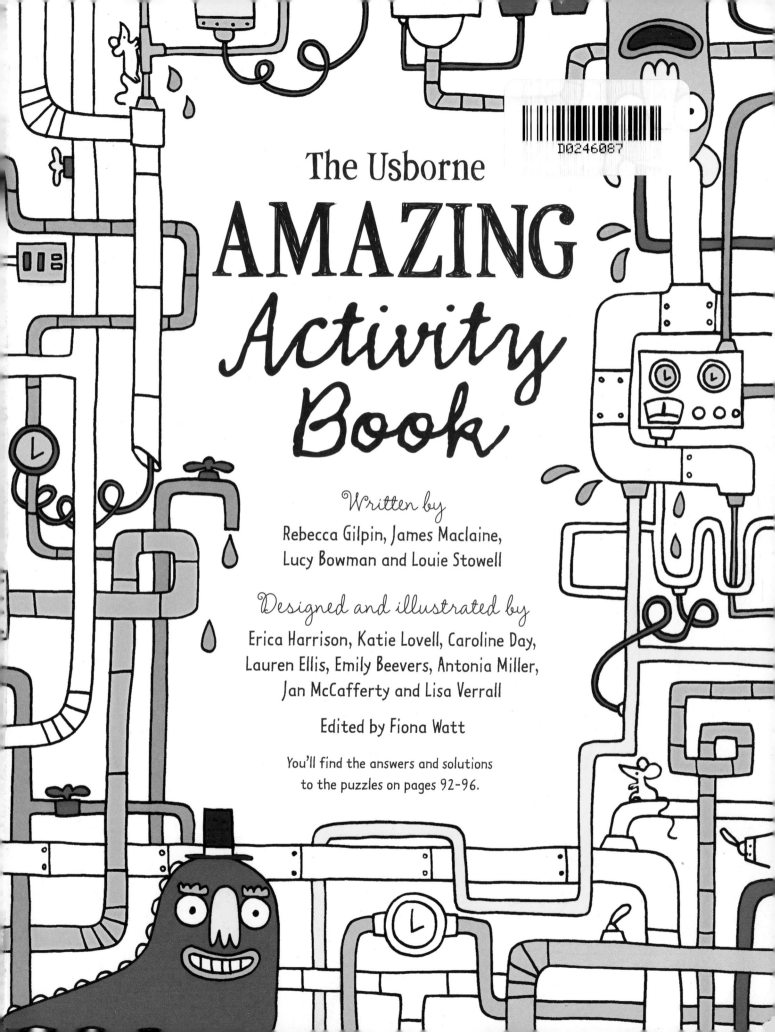

The Usborne
AMAZING
Activity Book

Written by

Rebecca Gilpin, James Maclaine,
Lucy Bowman and Louie Stowell

Designed and illustrated by

Erica Harrison, Katie Lovell, Caroline Day,
Lauren Ellis, Emily Beevers, Antonia Miller,
Jan McCafferty and Lisa Verrall

Edited by Fiona Watt

You'll find the answers and solutions
to the puzzles on pages 92-96.

FAIRGROUND FUN

The fair is in town. Sharpen your wits for these funfair puzzles.

WHO HIT IT?

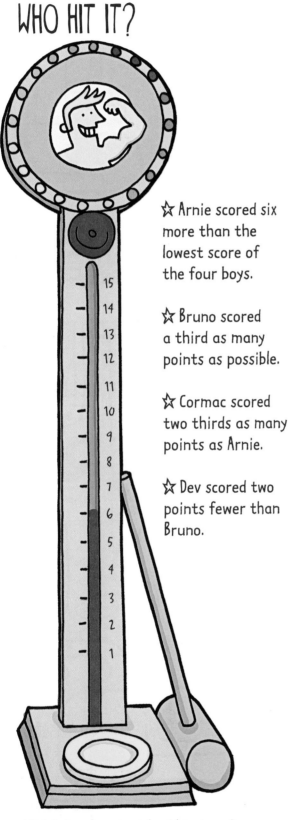

☆ Arnie scored six more than the lowest score of the four boys.

☆ Bruno scored a third as many points as possible.

☆ Cormac scored two thirds as many points as Arnie.

☆ Dev scored two points fewer than Bruno.

Which boy has just had his turn?

HIT THE CAN

In this game, each can's score is the sum of the two cans it stands on. Each can scores at least one point. Write on the missing scores, then figure out the total the boy will get, if he knocks down all the cans.

WORD DARTS

Each player must aim his dart at the card whose letters make a word when added to the letters on his back. Draw lines between the players and correct cards.

LOTS TO SPOT

It's a very busy day at the fair, but can you spot and circle:

☆ five people wearing sunglasses,
☆ someone taking a photo,
☆ one black bird,
☆ an upset little boy,
☆ five people wearing blue stripes,
☆ someone wearing purple boots
☆ and a girl who's not feeling well?

SNAKES AND LIZARDS

Doodle

lots of slithering snakes
and creeping lizards...

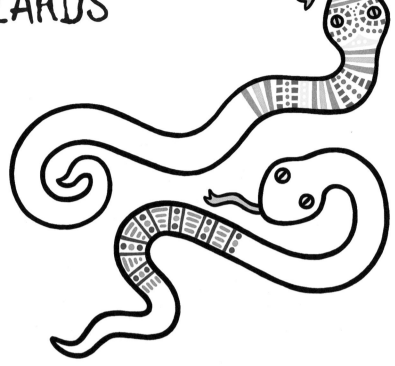

Fill these lizards
with patterns,
then draw
some more.

DID YOU KNOW?

sssssssnake puzzzzzzle

There are lots of snakes and snaky words hiding in this puzzle – see if you can find them all. They go up and down, across, and some are even backwards.

ANACONDA   COBRA   MAMBA   RATTLESNAKE   VENOM
BOA   FANGS   PYTHON   SCALES   VIPER

Cross the words off the list above as you find them.

D	F	A	S	E	L	A	C	S	Y	R	A	O	G	V	E	C	J	P	V
N	A	T	M	G	K	S	O	C	L	O	N	W	F	H	K	O	S	M	I
I	N	T	R	M	B	A	I	A	E	K	A	N	S	E	L	T	T	A	R
H	G	L	P	Z	O	N	F	J	F	M	K	O	E	M	I	Y	E	R	D
F	S	A	N	A	C	O	N	D	A	N	A	H	L	A	M	A	M	B	A
K	J	B	E	Q	E	M	S	B	N	L	T	T	A	P	R	O	Y	K	B
V	E	N	O	M	D	H	B	M	A	I	P	Y	K	S	G	N	O	H	O
R	O	L	O	C	O	B	R	A	X	M	U	P	R	E	P	I	V	L	A

THE GAME ZONE

Here are some fun games to play with your friends.

SLEEPY KNIGHTS

Play this somewhere you can lie down safely.

1. Choose someone to be the court jester. Everyone else is a sleepy knight. The knights lie still on the floor and pretend to be asleep.

2. The jester walks around between the knights and tries to get them to move by making them laugh.

He could make silly noises or tell a joke...

...but he's not allowed to touch the knights.

3. If a knight moves at all, he joins the jester and tries to make the other knights move. The last knight still sleeping is the winner.

WAKEY, WAKEY!

DRAW A ROBOT

Everyone needs a piece of paper and a pen.

1. Each person draws a robot's head on their paper.

2. Then they pass their paper to someone else, who adds a shape for a body.

3. Everyone keeps passing on their paper, adding something new each time.

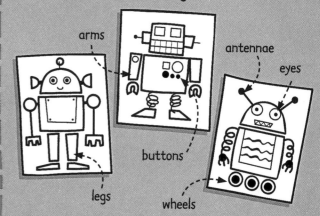

arms

antennae

eyes

buttons

legs

wheels

At the end, compare the different robot drawings.

6

FACE CHAIN

To play this, everyone has to be able to see each other's faces.

1. Someone makes a face, such as...

...an open mouth

2. The next person copies the face, then adds a new one of their own.

First... ...then

3. Everyone takes turns making all the faces in the correct order and adding their own.

If someone gets the order wrong or forgets a face, they're out.

PING BONG

1. You need a ball and someone to be the thrower. Everyone else has three lives.

Thrower

Everyone stands apart from each other.

2. The thrower throws the ball to someone, shouting either PING or BONG as they do it.

PING!

BONG!

...means catch the ball.

...means drop the ball.

The catcher has to do what the noise means. If they get it wrong, they lose one of their three lives.

3. The game continues with the thrower throwing to people at random, until only one other person is left.

FREEZE!

1. Choose someone to be a villain with an invisible freeze ray. He faces the wall and shouts...

GO!

Everyone else runs around behind him.

2. Suddenly, he turns around and shouts...

FREEZE!

Everyone has to stop, as if frozen to the spot. If the villain sees anyone move, they're out.

3. Everyone has to stay still until the villain faces the wall again and shouts "Go!"

4. The game continues until there's one person left. This person is the winner.

7

IN THE DARK

Doodle
bats, spiders, owls
and birds...

8

Which of these owls is the odd one out? Fill it in, then fill in the other owls, too...

1. 2. 3. 4.

5.

DID YOU KNOW?

Owls can't move their eyes, but if they want to see behind them, they can turn their heads all the way around.

Which of these flies gets eaten by the hungry bat?

A. B. C. D.

BRILLIANT BATS

Bats can 'see' using their ears! A bat makes lots of high squeaks as it flies. The squeaks hit things and bounce back off them. When a bat hears the squeaks, it knows it's found something.

This insect is about to be found – and eaten.

Rallies and races

This rally car needs to reach the finish line with as many points as possible. On the way, it encounters lots of challenges, and each challenge has a different number of points. It can only go through each challenge once. Can you figure out which route gives the car the most points?

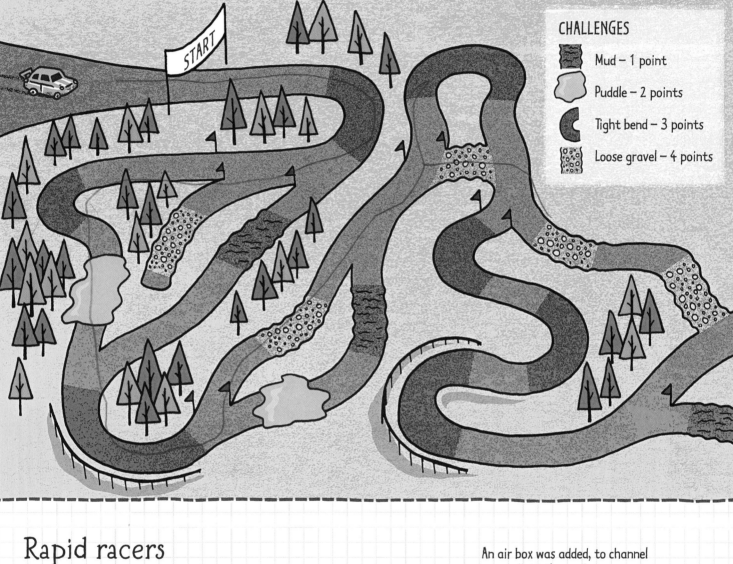

CHALLENGES

Mud – 1 point

Puddle – 2 points

Tight bend – 3 points

Loose gravel – 4 points

Rapid racers

See how race car designs have changed over time...

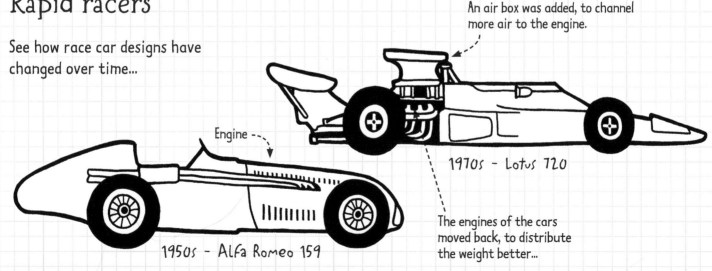

An air box was added, to channel more air to the engine.

Engine

1970s – Lotus 720

1950s – Alfa Romeo 159

The engines of the cars moved back, to distribute the weight better...

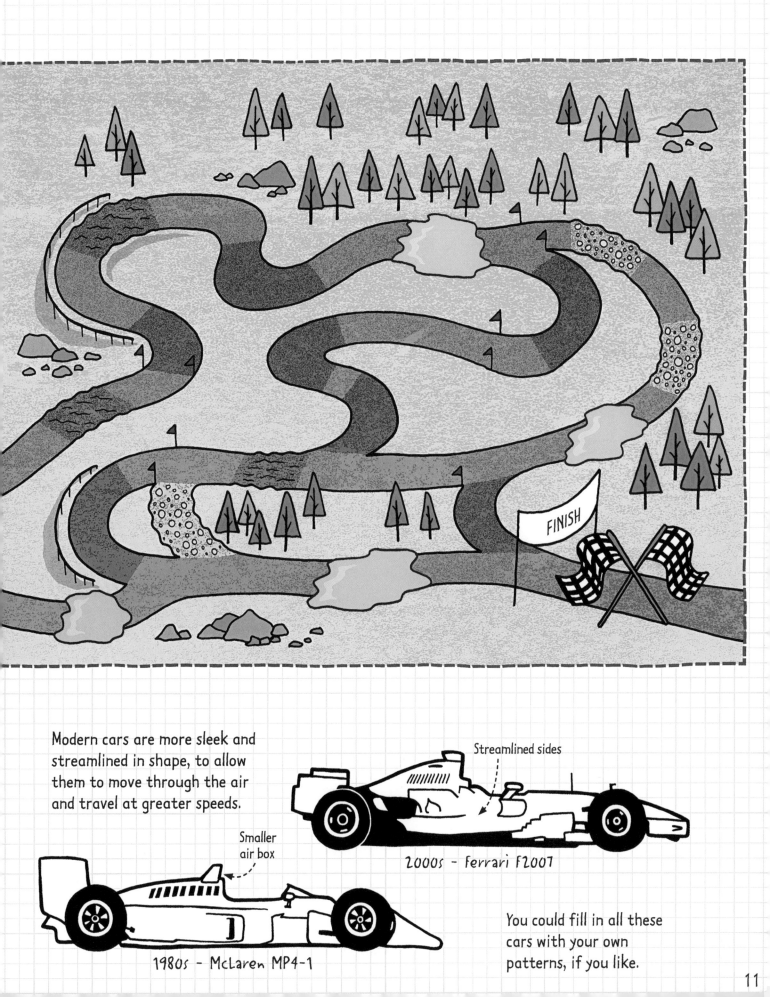

Modern cars are more sleek and streamlined in shape, to allow them to move through the air and travel at greater speeds.

Streamlined sides

2000s - Ferrari F2007

Smaller air box

1980s - McLaren MP4-1

You could fill in all these cars with your own patterns, if you like.

IN THE WILD WEST

The Sheriff wants a word with Cowboy Bill, and Cowboy Bill isn't happy. The people of the town have taken cover – they've seen this kind of thing before. Can you see fifteen people watching what's going on? Fill them in as you find them.

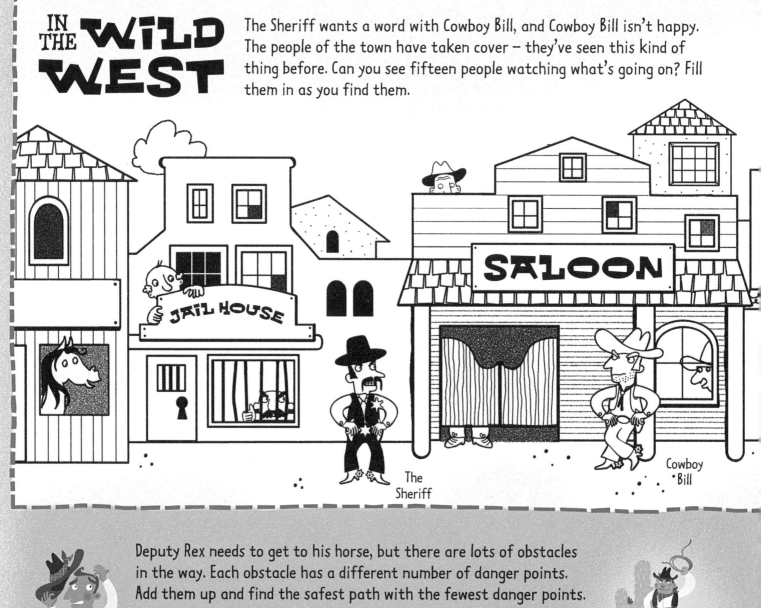

JAIL HOUSE

SALOON

The Sheriff

Cowboy Bill

Deputy Rex needs to get to his horse, but there are lots of obstacles in the way. Each obstacle has a different number of danger points. Add them up and find the safest path with the fewest danger points.

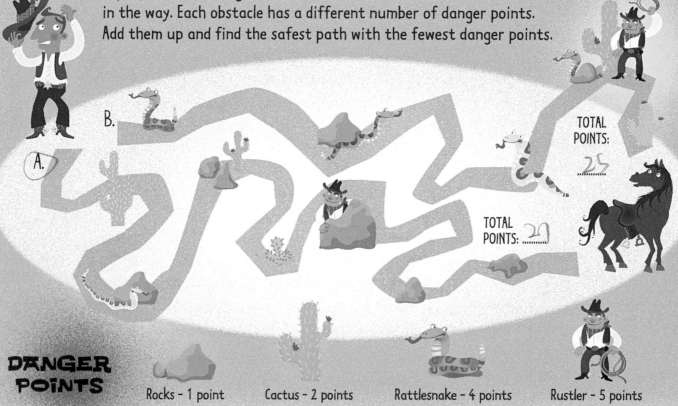

B.

A.

TOTAL POINTS: 25

TOTAL POINTS: 20

DANGER POINTS

Rocks - 1 point   Cactus - 2 points   Rattlesnake - 4 points   Rustler - 5 points

12

There's a horse rustler on the loose who needs to be caught. The poster on the left is pinned up in town, but there are four mistakes on the other one – can you spot them?

Street sports

Doodle
more free runners leaping and tumbling...

Some ideas:

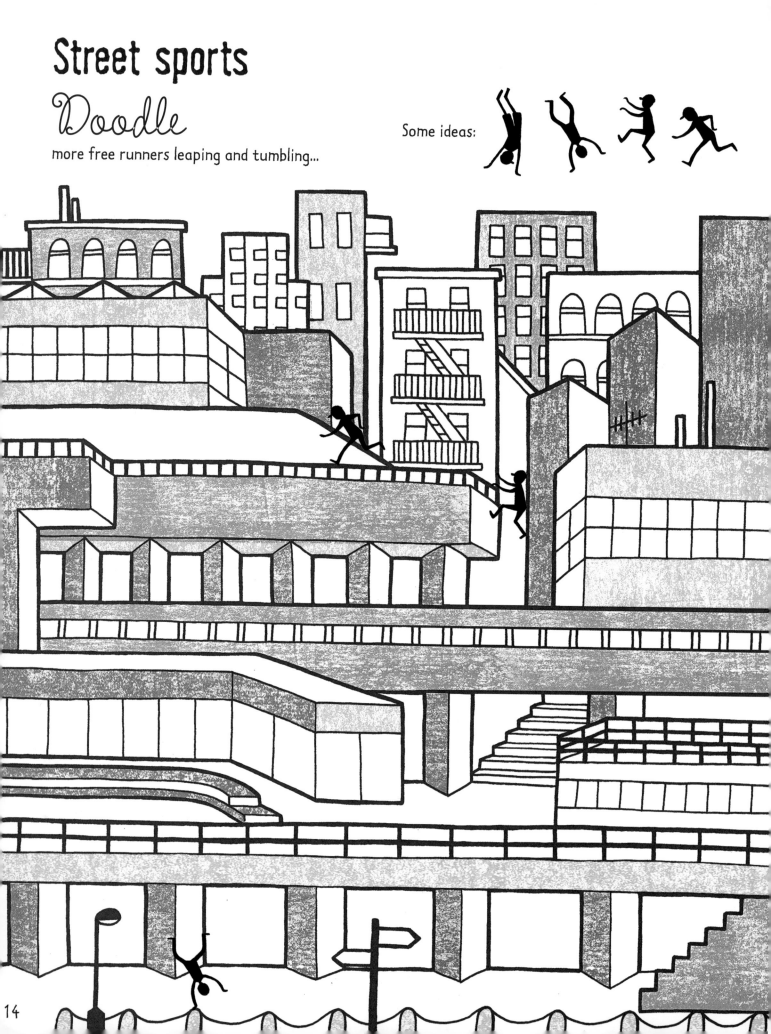

At the skate park

Down at the skate park there's lots going on – see if you can spot the following:

☆ 4 BMX riders   ☆ 1 small, red ball   ☆ 2 people eating ice cream

☆ 8 skateboards   ☆ 2 boys wearing caps

Design your own skateboard

Draw designs and patterns on these skateboards, and fill in the wheels:

HEROES...

The descriptions of these heroes and villains are jumbled up across the pages. Read them carefully, and then draw a line from each description to the correct picture.

A.

The courageous Norse hero **Sigurd** grew up to kill the dragon Fafnir. He could also talk to birds.

B.

The gigantic creature **Grendel** appeared in the poem *Beowulf*. At night, he attacked and ate people.

C.

Set was the Ancient Egyptian god of chaos, storms and the desert. He was also very evil. He murdered his own brother Osiris.

D.

The villainous pirate **Edward "Blackbeard" Teach** was a whole head taller than most men. His nickname came from his huge black beard. He used to go into battle with several burning fuses woven into his hair.

E.

Hello!

Hi!

Count Dracula was created by the Irish writer Bram Stoker. This vampire bit his victims and drank their blood. He could climb walls like a lizard and change his body shape at will.

AND VILLAINS...

F.

Hercules was the strongest and bravest Greek hero. He was set twelve near-impossible tasks by a king named Eurystheus. Armed with a club, he killed many terrifying monsters.

Sinbad the Sailor was the swashbuckling hero of several Middle Eastern adventure stories. On his travels, Sinbad survived many dangers, from stormy seas to giant snakes.

G.

The Chinese monkey king **Sun Wukong** had impressive superpowers. He was famed for his supernatural speed, strength and ability to change shape.

H.

I.

The legendary British ruler **King Arthur** was renowned for his bravery and battle skills. His sword was named Excalibur, and his comrades were known as the Knights of the Round Table.

Dinosaur land

Add lots of dinosaur stickers from the sticker pages to this prehistoric landscape.

Number crunching

Cracking crocodile

Follow the instructions to work out how many teeth the baby crocodile should have. Then, draw them on.

Cross out:

☆ even numbers

☆ the total number of sides three triangles have

☆ numbers less than six

☆ the number of days in a week

☆ the answer to eight plus seven

Kayak race

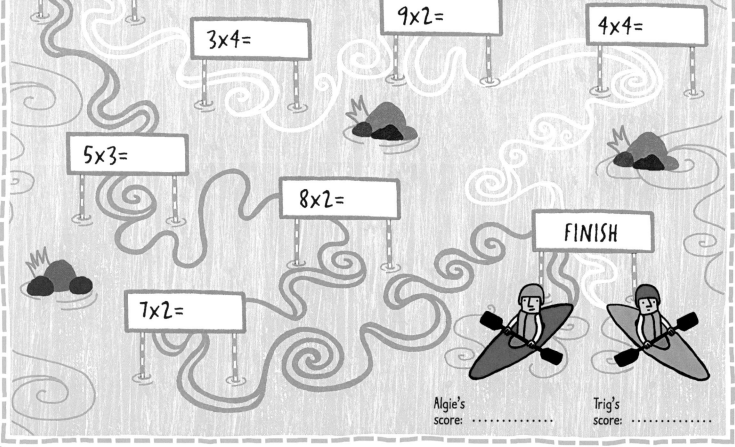

Algie and Trig have just finished a kayak race. Solve the problem on each gate to work out how many points each one got for paddling through it. Who got the most points and won the race?

START

3x4=

9x2=

4x4=

5x3=

8x2=

FINISH

7x2=

Algie's score: . . . .

Trig's score: . . . .

Keypad code

Look at the phone and work out the code, to reveal the message!

1x8 2x4 2x3   3x2 3x6 1x3 2x3   2x6 2x8 1x6 2x2 2x3 3x7
T   H   E

3x4 4x7   3x3 3x4 3x3 1x8 3x9   4x7 2x3 3x8 2x3 2x6.

Now, try writing out the rest of this message in the code:

M E E T   A T   N O O N.

1x6

Clue: the first word has been decoded for you.

1	2 abc	3 def
4 ghi	5 jkl	6 mno
7 pqrs	8 tuv	9 wxyz
+	0	#

Animal numbers

Can you spot the numbers hidden in these pictures?

From 1 to 100

Can you find the way through this maze of numbers from square 1 to 100? You can move up, down, left and right, but only to a square with a higher number on it.

1	22	5	3	68	71	73	74	16
9	11	10	64	66	60	57	76	63
8	14	13	59	52	56	53	80	62
18	15	12	58	55	40	48	81	82
20	29	27	31	49	47	54	45	87
23	28	34	38	41	37	92	90	89
25	24	30	40	39	61	93	88	85
26	43	35	37	42	77	94	98	100

DID YOU KNOW?

One followed by 100 zeroes is called a googol. The name was coined by a mathematician's nine-year-old nephew in 1938.

A googol!

1,000000 0000000000000000000

00000000000000000000

MONSTER DOODLES

Using a black pen, turn these shapes into monsters...
Add horns, eyes and fang-filled mouths!

ROBOTS

ROBOT FACTORY

Which button will turn on the light in the middle of this robot's control panel?

To reveal the robot in this puzzle, fill in the shapes with a dot in them:

The robot factory has run out of parts... The top robot in this line is finished – can you finish off the others?

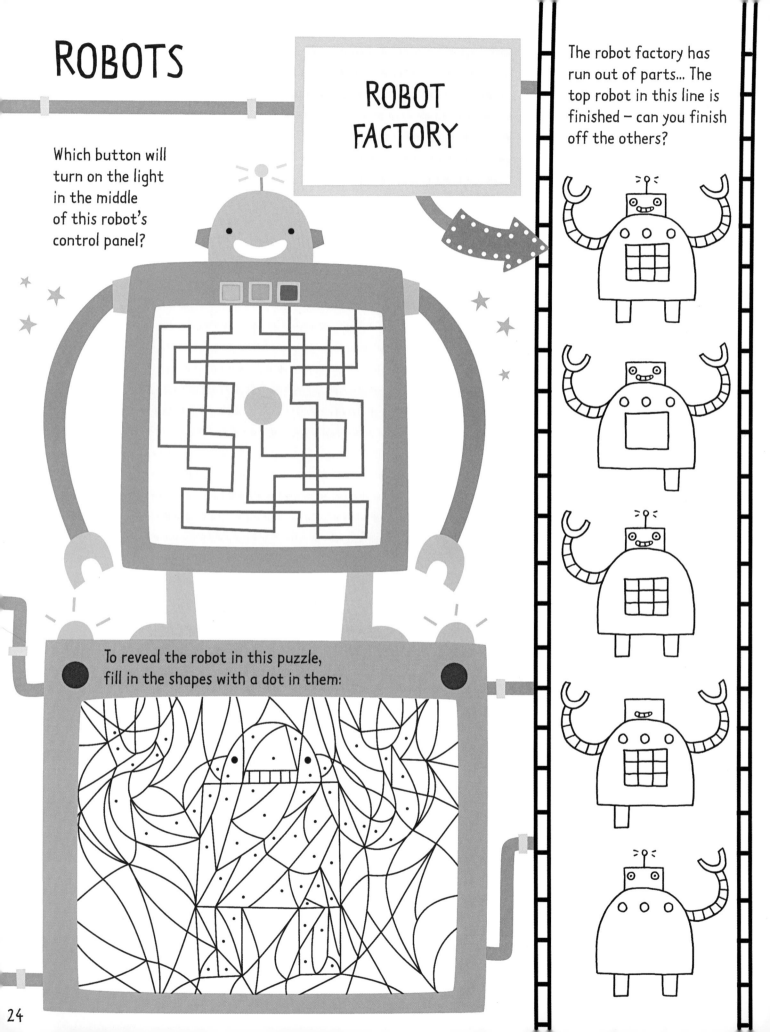

PAPER ROBOT

Follow these steps to make a robot from a rectangular piece of paper...

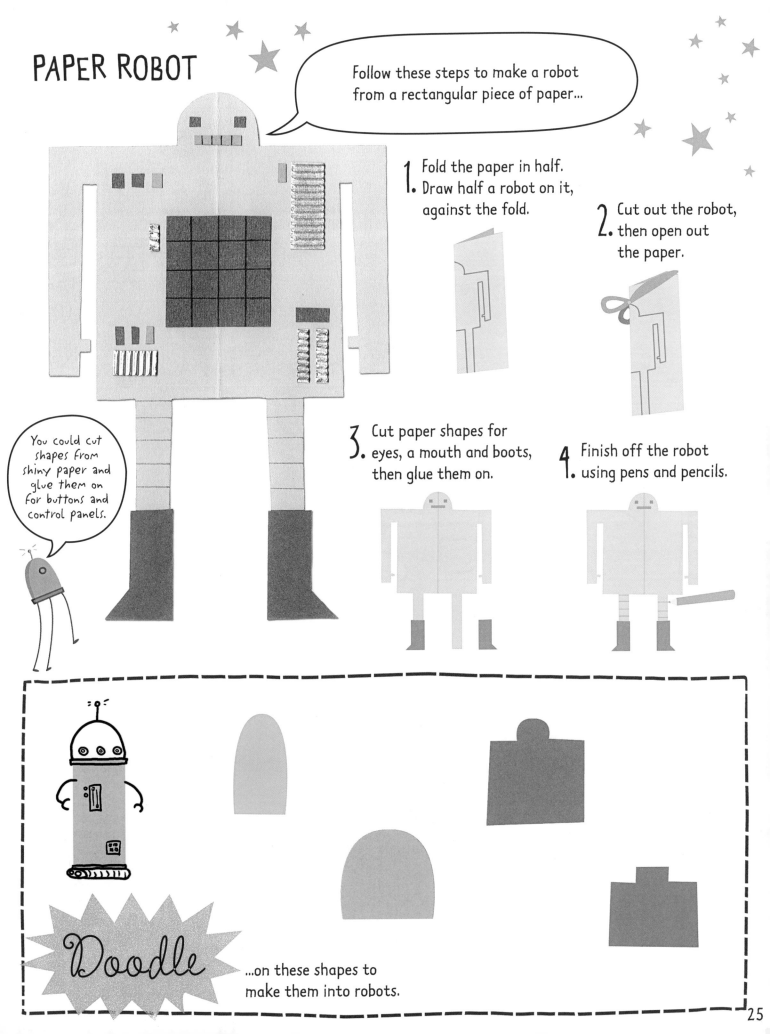

1. Fold the paper in half. Draw half a robot on it, against the fold.

2. Cut out the robot, then open out the paper.

You could cut shapes from shiny paper and glue them on for buttons and control panels.

3. Cut paper shapes for eyes, a mouth and boots, then glue them on.

4. Finish off the robot using pens and pencils.

Doodle

...on these shapes to make them into robots.

JUNGLE ESCAPE

This explorer is deep in the jungle, facing all kinds of danger. Keeping to the paths at all times, help him to find a safe route to the village, avoiding all the perils in his way... including hungry piranhas, lethal snakes, and vicious stinging fire ants.

GRRRR!

AT THE MATCH

It's match day and the stadium's full of cheering fans. Can you circle the three Rivington Reds' fans sitting in the Blakeley Blues' stand?

MATCHING PAIRS

The players' socks have been jumbled up. Draw lines between the pairs, and circle the odd sock.

Can you divide the circle into seven parts using just three straight lines?

TROPHY TROUBLE

Look closely at the trophies and circle the odd one out.

1.   2.   3.   4.

KICKAROUND

These players can only pass the ball up, down, left or right, to any of the players nearest to them. Each player's number shows how many times he touches the ball. Draw lines from player to player showing who kicks the ball to whom.

This player passes the ball first.

1 2
2 4 6 2
2 3 4 2

HA HA HA

Q. What percentage of goalkeepers can jump higher than the crossbar?

A. 100%. The crossbar can't jump!

★ FINISH THE STORY

Here's the beginning of a story about a boy who is sent a mysterious gift in the mail that promises to give him superpowers. What do you think happens next? Finish the story using the questions on the right to help you.

...WHOOSH!

Before you start writing, ask yourself...

- What happens next?

- What does Jed decide to do with his new powers?

- Does anything go wrong?

- Does Jed find out who sent him the package?

- Does he face any evil villains?

- Does Jed keep the ring at the end of the story and become a superhero?

Add a title for your story here...

There once was an inquisitive boy named Jed, who lived in an ordinary town with his ordinary parents. One rainy day, something very out of the ordinary happened...

A strange-looking package arrived for him. The wrapping seemed to glow slightly and the package was closed with a blob of fluorescent wax.

When Jed opened the mysterious package, he found a ring inside. It was silver with twisted patterns on it, and it looked very expensive. With the ring was a note:

This magical ring gives the person who wears it superhuman strength and the power to fly. Do you dare to put it on your finger?

Jed couldn't resist. He slipped the ring onto his finger and...

Continue the story here...

UNDERGROUND LAIR
challenge
hover Supervillain
RESCUE FREEZE RAY
HAZARDOUS
invisible ZOOM
POWERFUL
★
whirl DESTINY
EVIL SCHEME
daring

You could use some of these words in your story if you like.

KAPOW!

BOOM!

DESIGN YOUR OWN
SUPERHERO COSTUME

In the shadows

Shadow show

1. Shine a spotlight onto a white wall. Make sure all the other lights in the room are switched off.

2. Make shapes with your hands in front of the light to cast shadows onto the wall.

Flap your hands to see the bird beat its wings.

Try making these animal-shaped shadows with your hands:

Open and close your little fingers, to make the dog bark.

Put two strips of paper between your fingers to make the snake's tongue.

Make the rabbit's ears twitch by wiggling your fingers.

Flick your fingers, to bend the elephant's trunk.

Snap your hands - or the crocodile's mouth - shut.

Shape up

A triangular shadow is blocking out some of the letters in this list of shapes. Fill in the missing letters.

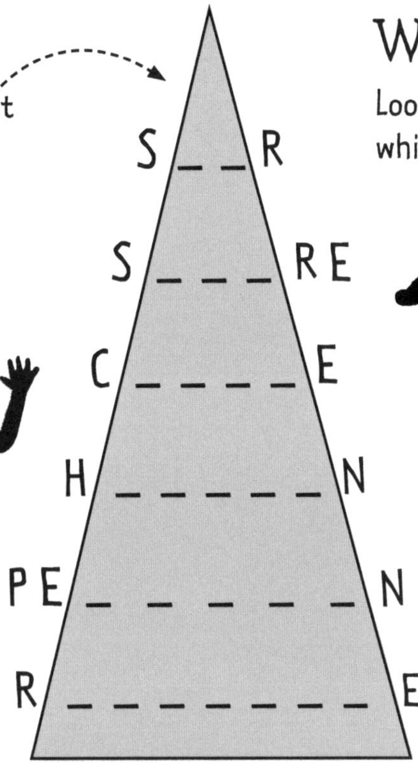

S _ _ R
S _ _ _ R E
C _ _ _ _ E
H _ _ _ _ N
P E _ _ _ _ _ N
R _ _ _ _ _ E

DID YOU KNOW?

Your shadow is longest at sunrise and sunset and shortest at midday. Can you guess why?

Which car?

Look at these cars carefully. Can you see which one matches the black shape?

Odd one out

Circle the odd one out.

Famous buildings

Draw a line between each building's silhouette and its correct name.

ANGKOR WAT

SYDNEY OPERA HOUSE

TOWER BRIDGE

COLOSSEUM

GOLDEN GATE BRIDGE

TAJ MAHAL

EIFFEL TOWER

EMPIRE STATE BUILDING

WHIZZING WHEELS

At the track

Draw cars whizzing around this racetrack:

Draw more curved shapes like this for crash barriers.

Find the wheels...

This car needs a new set of wheels. Can you find four identical ones here?

You could add oil slicks like this and loose pebbles on the track.

Symmetry puzzle

Something that's symmetrical can be divided in half using a straight line, and each half is an exact reflection of the other. Which of these car parts are symmetrical, and which aren't? Write 'Yes' below each symmetrical part and 'No' below the others. The first one has been done, to get you started:

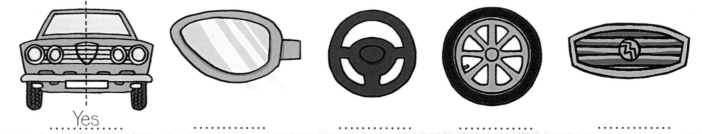

Yes

Mixed-up plates

Can you unscramble these jumbled letters to find car-related words?

MORRRIS

....

EDEPS

....

KERABS

....

EENING

....

LESHEW

....

Quick exit

A getaway car has sped away from the scene of a crime, leaving a clear print in the mud.

Which of the cars below was the getaway car?

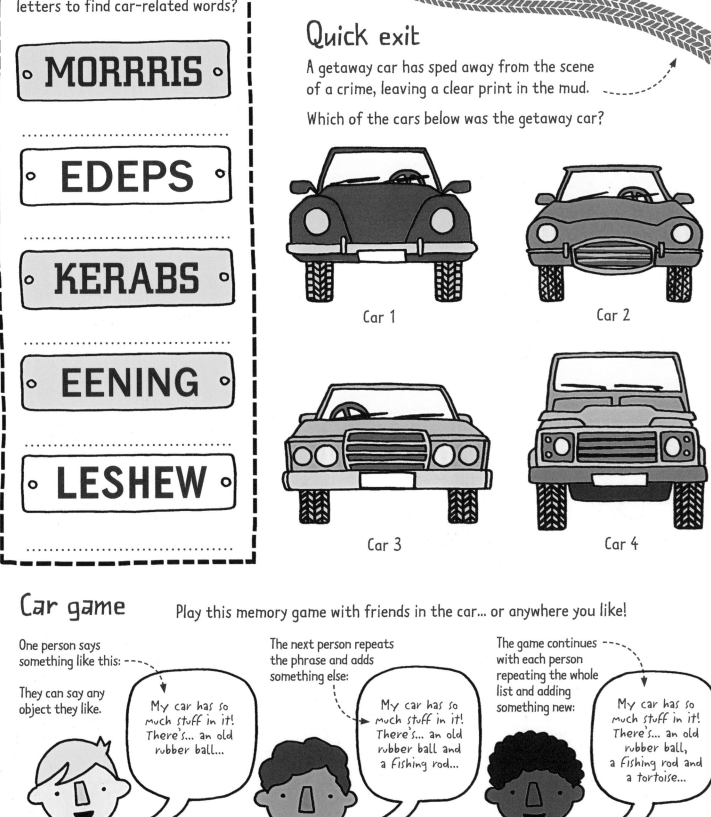

Car 1

Car 2

Car 3

Car 4

Car game

Play this memory game with friends in the car... or anywhere you like!

One person says something like this:

They can say any object they like.

My car has so much stuff in it! There's... an old rubber ball...

The next person repeats the phrase and adds something else:

My car has so much stuff in it! There's... an old rubber ball and a fishing rod...

The game continues with each person repeating the whole list and adding something new:

My car has so much stuff in it! There's... an old rubber ball, a fishing rod and a tortoise...

If someone forgets something, or says the wrong thing, they're out – and the last person still playing wins.

BON APPÉTIT

GET DIPPING

It's very easy to make dips for vegetable sticks and tortilla chips. Here's how...

Spicy salsa
You'll need:

Chop me finely...

...and us too.

½ a red onion

3 tomatoes

Some coriander (cilantro) leaves

Squeeze me!

I'm hot!

½ a lime

One or two drops of hot pepper sauce

1. Mix all the ingredients together with the lime juice.

2. Dip and eat!

Guacamole
You'll need:

Remove my skin and stone (pit)!

Squeeze me!

1 avocado

½ a lime

Crush me!

1 garlic clove

2 teaspoons of olive oil

1 tablespoon of plain yogurt

1. Mash an avocado with a fork and mix in the lime juice.

2. Add the garlic, oil and yogurt. Mix well.

MONSTER FOOD Draw monster faces on the food.

Can you work out which chef has cooked the most meatballs?

A.   B.   C.   D.

Who forgot to make any meatballs?

Shopping list

Can you continue filling this shopping list with the names of different foods? Each food should begin with the last letter of the food before it.

TOMATO-OLIVES-SOUP-PASTA-APPLES-

DID YOU KNOW?

☆ The Ancient Romans seasoned their meals with a peculiar sauce called garum. It was made from rotting fish guts.

☆ If you shake and shake a jar two thirds full of cream, you'll eventually make butter.

☆ The first chocolate bars were made in 1847 by Francis Fry.

☆ The white truffle is one of the most expensive items of food in the world. In 2007, a single truffle sold for $330,000 (£165,000).

☆ The German cheese Milbenkäse is made with tiny living creatures called cheese mites.

cheese mite*

*not actual size!

PIZZA PUZZLE

The number of mushrooms and pepperoni pieces on each slice follows a certain sequence. Figure it out, and draw the right number of toppings on the fourth slice!

Move in this direction...

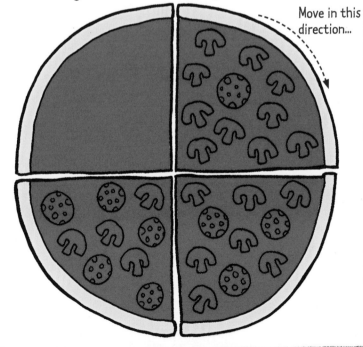

37

BURIED TREASURE HUNT

Follow the directions below to find the pirates' buried treasure. Then, cover the map with stickers of ships, fish and sea monsters from the sticker pages.

Sail east up to the rocks then turn south and keep sailing, but stop just before the whirlpool. Travel eastward until you're exactly between a Point and a Head. Then, sail directly north until you reach land. On this island, mark a line between the two mountains. Draw another between the pool and palm trees. Where the lines cross, you can dig for gold!

Start here... and stick the small ship stickers along the route.

Skull Shore

Can you spot a red parrot?

Crab Beach

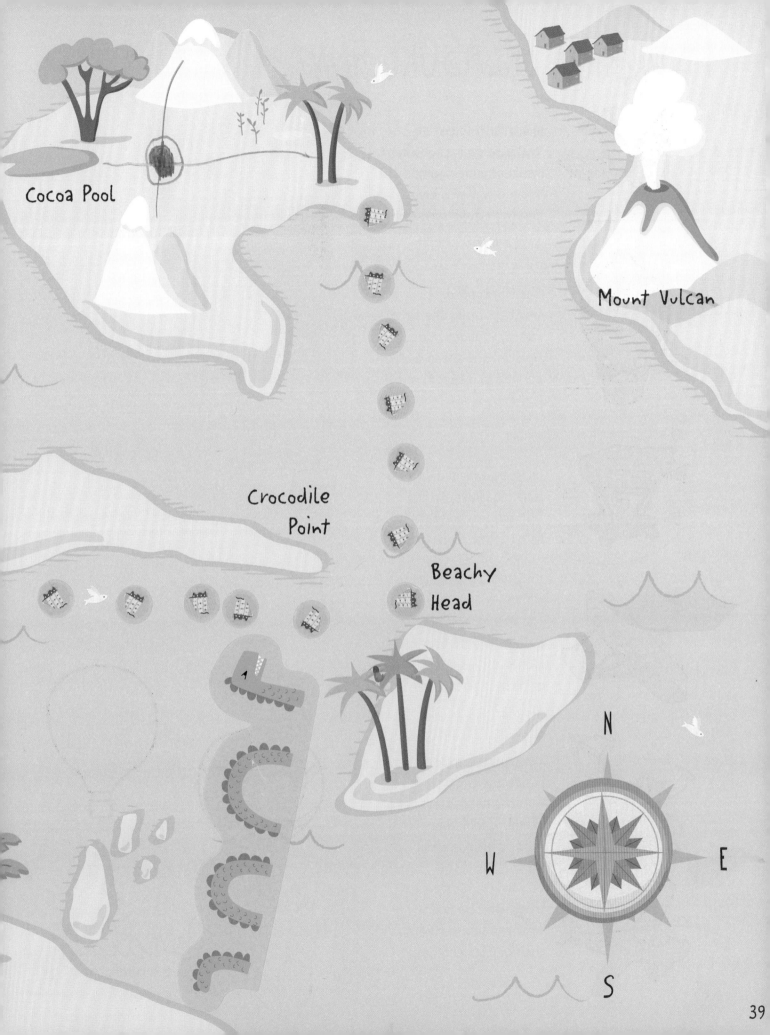

Cocoa Pool

Mount Vulcan

Crocodile
Point

Beachy
Head

N

W

E

S

Flying high

TIMELINE

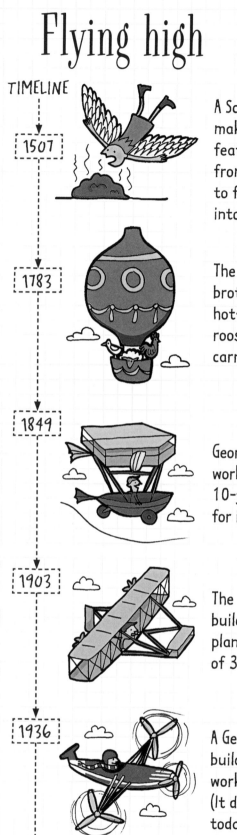

1507
A Scottish scientist makes a pair of chicken feather wings, jumps from a wall and tries to fly. He falls straight into a pile of dung.

1783
The Montgolfier brothers build the first hot-air balloon. A duck, rooster and sheep are carried in a test flight.

1849
George Cayley builds a working glider. A 10-year-old boy takes it for its first flight.

1903
The Wright brothers build the first powered plane. It flies a distance of 37m (120ft).

1936
A German scientist builds the first working helicopter. (It didn't look like today's helicopters.)

1930s
Frank Whittle and Hans von Ohain invent the first jet engines.

Doodle
more hot-air balloons.

40

Make a paper plane

Follow these steps to make a plane from a rectangular piece of paper.

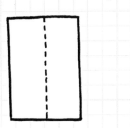 1. Fold, and reopen.

2. Fold in the corners.

Fold along here.... 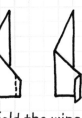 ...and here.

3. Fold them over again.

 4. Fold the plane in half.

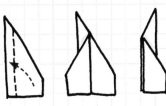 5. Fold back the sides to make the wings.

 6. Fold the wing tips over, to make your plane go faster.

Now, throw your plane and watch it fly.

Flight plan

Can you help the Peregrine Airways' pilot fly his plane back to the airport in Falconia? He has to follow the available flight routes, flying from airport to airport. But, he doesn't have permission to land in the countries shown in green on the map below...

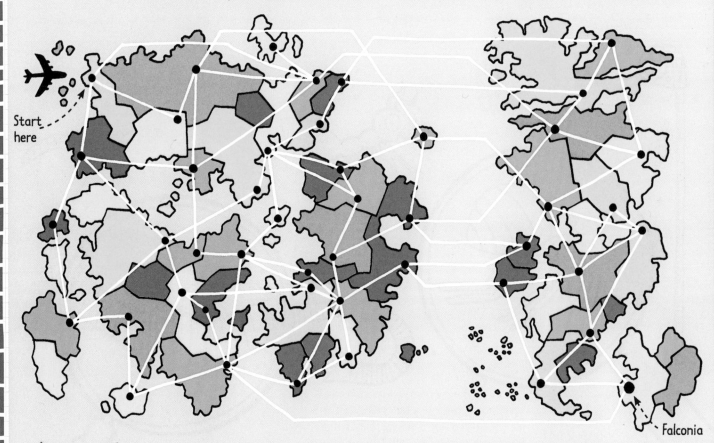

Start here

Falconia

CREEPY-CRAWLIES

SILLY GAME

...Ask a friend any question...

What do you like to eat?

CREEPY-CRAWLIES!

...and the answer is:

What's on my nose?

CREEPY-CRAWLIES!

Take turns to ask questions – the answer is always the same!

What do you put on salad?

CREEPY-CRAWLIES!

Anyone who laughs is out of the game.

Doodle more bugs in this space...

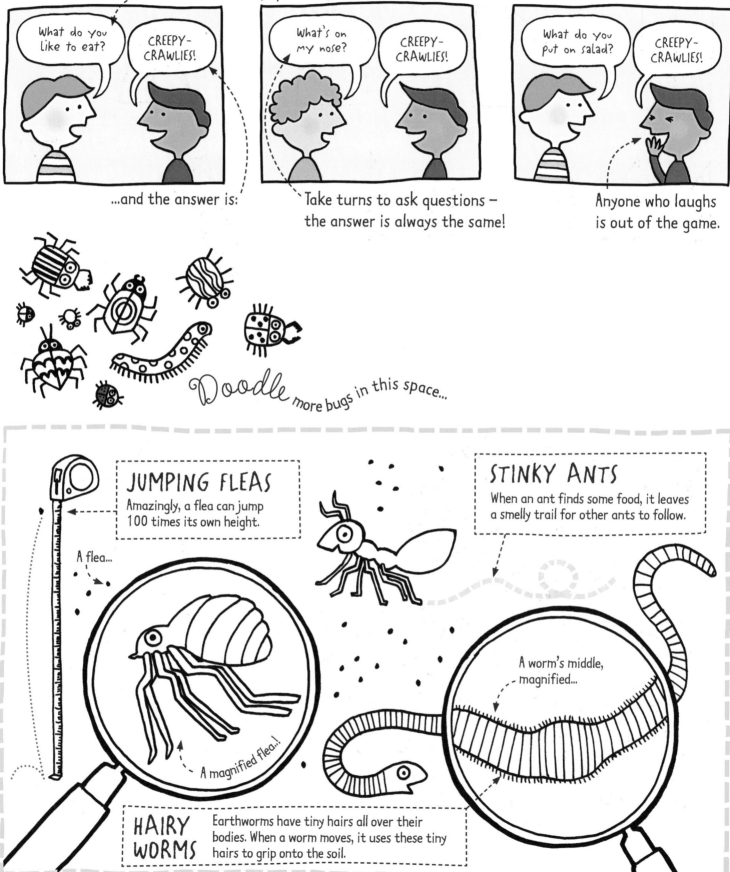

JUMPING FLEAS
Amazingly, a flea can jump 100 times its own height.

A flea...

A magnified flea...

STINKY ANTS
When an ant finds some food, it leaves a smelly trail for other ants to follow.

A worm's middle, magnified...

HAIRY WORMS
Earthworms have tiny hairs all over their bodies. When a worm moves, it uses these tiny hairs to grip onto the soil.

SPIDER QUIZ

1. How many eyes do most spiders have?

....

2. Do spiders have bones?

....

3. Spiders have pale blue blood – TRUE or FALSE?

....

4. What are the biggest kind of spiders?

....

5. Spiders have fangs – TRUE or FALSE?

....

Doodle
more spiders and flies...

NAME GAME

Say aloud what each picture on the left is of, then try doing the same with the pictures on the right... (You'll find it much harder!)

dragonfly	snail	ant
slug	beetle	caterpillar
fly	spider	worm

beetle	worm	slug
fly	dragonfly	spider
snail	caterpillar	ant

43

Exploring Earth

Read the descriptions of these four great explorers below. Then, look closely and circle four things that shouldn't be in the pictures.

Englishman Captain Cook explored the coastline of Australia in the 1770s.

In 1911, Norwegian Roald Amundsen and his team became the first people to reach the South Pole.

Venetian explorer Marco Polo set sail for Asia in 1271.

Viking explorer Leif Ericsson sailed to North America in the year 1000.

DID YOU KNOW?

In the Middle Ages, the little-explored Atlantic Ocean was sometimes known as the Green Sea of Darkness. Sailors were afraid that if they went too far, they'd never find their way back.

Where on Earth am I?

Due east

How many times can you find the word 'east' in this puzzle?

It could be written horizontally or vertically and may be backwards.

```
      E A E S E
    E S A A A E E
  A S T E S A S A E
S T S T E T E A S T A
A E T E S E E A E S E
E A T S E T A E S E T
E S S T S A E A E A S
T T A E S T E T A S T
S E E A E S S E T
  E A T S A E A
    E E S A E
```

ARCTIC ANIMAL ADVENTURE

Guide the explorer in his kayak through the ice, taking him past as many different Arctic animals as possible. Don't paddle along the same route twice and try to avoid any dead ends.

FINISH

SPACE STUFF

Balloon rocket

To make a balloon rocket, you'll need:

a long piece of thread   3m (10ft)   a drinking straw   a long balloon   sticky tape   2 chairs   a large clip

Pull the chairs apart until the thread is stretched tight.

1. Push the thread through the straw, then tie the thread to the chairs.

2. Blow up the balloon, twist its end and clip the end tightly. Tape the balloon onto the straw...

3. ...then pull the clipped end of the balloon rocket to one end of the thread.

4. Quickly remove the clip to release the balloon rocket and see what happens.

PLANETS QUIZ

1. Which planet is closest to the Sun?
   A. Jupiter   B. Earth   C. Mercury

2. Which planet has lots of bright rings around it?
   A. Mercury   B. Saturn   C. Venus

3. Which is the largest planet?
   A. Earth   B. Jupiter   C. Mars

4. Which planet looks brightest from Earth?
   A. Venus   B. Neptune   C. Uranus

5. Which planet is named after the Roman god of the sea?
   A. Saturn   B. Mars   C. Neptune

MISSION CONTROL LOGBOOK

Imagine you're being sent on a space mission... Before you set off, you need to write the details of your mission in this logbook:

CAPTAIN: ....

CREW: ....

....

SPACECRAFT: ....

DESTINATION: ....

JOURNEY TIME: ....

EQUIPMENT: ....

....

Doodle

...lots of stars and planets.

Add rockets, too...

...and some shooting stars!

WORDSEARCH

Find these words in the big planet on the right — they go horizontally or vertically, and some may even be backwards.

SATELLITE   COMET   ASTEROID

SUN   GALAXY   EARTH

UNIVERSE   ROCKET   MOON

SPACECRAFT

```
                      E   E
          O   N   L   T   T
          A   R   O   L   I   I
    S   U   S   D   O   A   K   L
    P   N   P   C   M   S   A   L
    M   O   I   A   T   I   T   E   E
    R   G   E   U   C   O   M   E   T   T
    E   E   A   R   M   E   O   V   R   T   A
E   A   L   L   I   P   C   O   M   O   U   S
A   B   U   A   E   S   R   E   V   I   N   U
O   R   E   M   X   U   G   A   L   M   D   I   M
U   T   I   D   Y   N   V   F   E   A   K   N   X
S   H   R   O   C   K   E   T   U   C   S   U   N
```

47

BIG BATTLE

There are lots of things to spot and circle in this busy battle scene and space for you to draw your own soldiers and horses, too.

Which five soldiers have lost their helmets?

Can you spot the soldier with an arrow in his eye?

Which soldier has had his head cut off?

Which soldier has lost an arm?

Can you spot two snapped lances?

Can you find four birds in danger?

Which archer has run out of arrows?

HOW TO DRAW A SOLDIER...

DINOSAUR LAND
Pages 18-19

BURIED TREASURE HUNT
Pages 38-39

Use these small ship stickers to mark the ship's route to the buried treasure.

SPACE WALK
Pages 56-57

ANCIENT EGYPT
Page 66

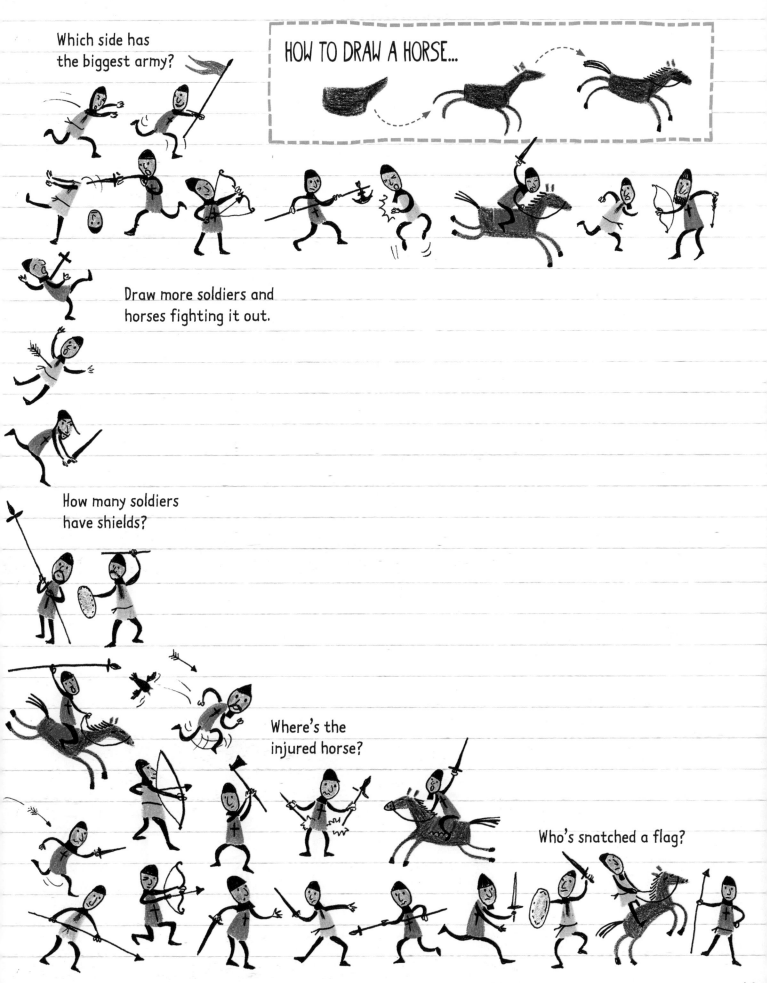

Which side has the biggest army?

HOW TO DRAW A HORSE...

Draw more soldiers and horses fighting it out.

How many soldiers have shields?

Where's the injured horse?

Who's snatched a flag?

CROOKED CRIMINALS
WHODUNNIT?

Can you help the police work out who's guilty from these clues? The culprit...

☆ has big, bushy eyebrows
☆ has dark hair
☆ has been injured

☆ has a pierced ear or nose
☆ is a birdwatcher

A.　　B.　　C.　　D.　　E.

DUSTING FOR PRINTS

Follow these easy steps to dust for fingerprints...

1. Make a fingerprint on a glass surface.

2. Gently brush some talcum powder onto it.

3. Press on some sticky tape, and peel it off.

50

SPOT THE DIFFERENCE

Nothing is safe when there's a burglar around! Can you spot and circle the five things he's stolen from this room... and one thing of his that he's left behind?

BEFORE

AFTER

COPS AND ROBBERS

Turn these fingerprints into cops and robbers.

Under the sea

The diver has taken photos of sea creatures, but he's left his camera in zoom mode, and the photos are too close up. Which creatures has he photographed? When you've spotted each creature in the main picture, fill it in.

How to avoid a shark attack

Read the tips in the picture below, to find out how best to avoid dangerous sharks when swimming in the sea.

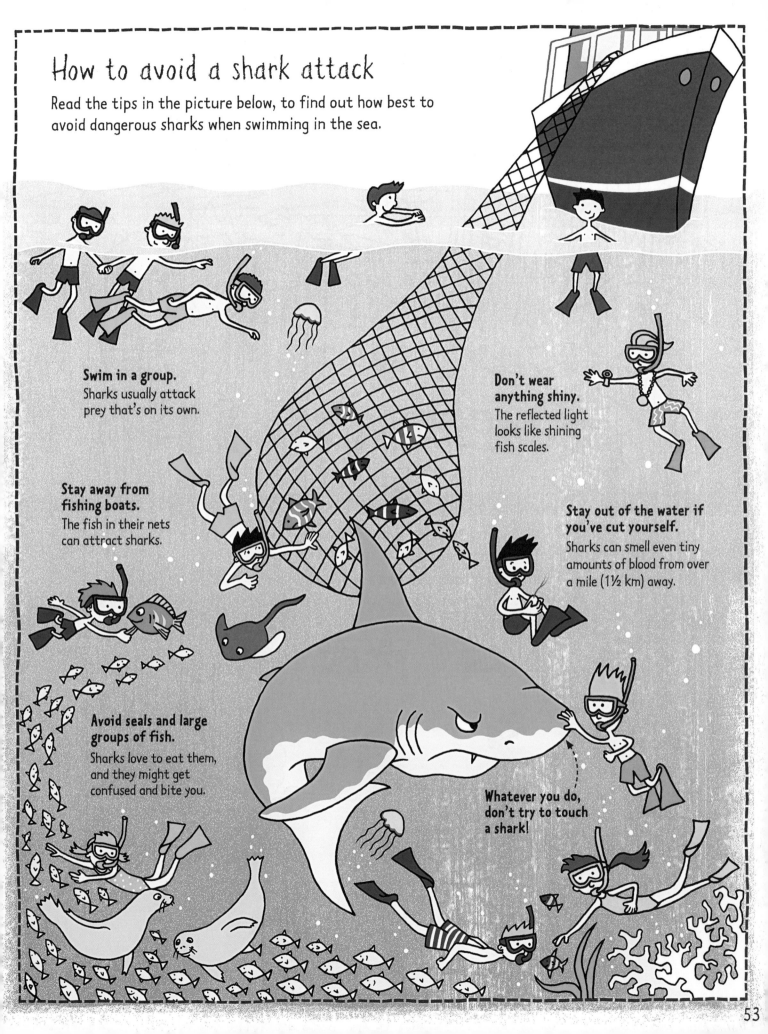

Swim in a group.
Sharks usually attack prey that's on its own.

Stay away from fishing boats.
The fish in their nets can attract sharks.

Avoid seals and large groups of fish.
Sharks love to eat them, and they might get confused and bite you.

Don't wear anything shiny.
The reflected light looks like shining fish scales.

Stay out of the water if you've cut yourself.
Sharks can smell even tiny amounts of blood from over a mile (1½ km) away.

Whatever you do, don't try to touch a shark!

The great outdoors

Bug search

Fifteen creepy-crawlies are hiding in this picture. Find them and fill them in.

Leaving messages

Oops! Calum has overslept. His friends have gone exploring, leaving him behind in the tent. They've left him a message, using twigs and stones, showing which way to go. Use the key below to decode the message and find where Calum should go.

KEY

Take the first right

Take the first left

Go straight ahead

Climb over a gate

Go over stepping stones

Jamal and Dave are lost in a forest. Can you help them find a safe way back to their van? Watch out for nasty creatures and other dangers along the way...

BEWARE! QUICKSAND

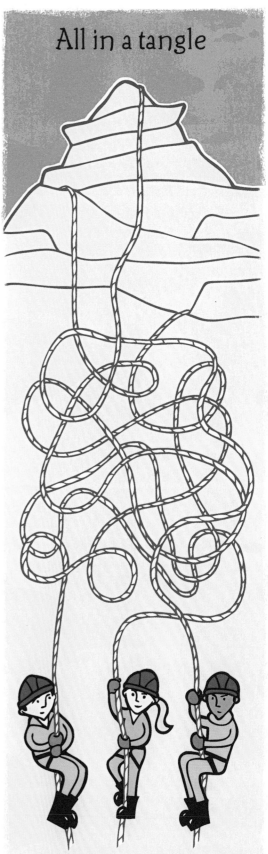

All in a tangle

Three climbers are really excited about climbing up Craggy Mountain. Unfortunately, their ropes are in a mess. Can you find out which climber gets to the top?

55

Space walk

An astronaut needs to go on a space walk, to make urgent repairs to a satellite. First, add lots of stickers from the sticker pages. Then, without taking your pen off the pages, draw a looping route from the astronaut to the satellite. Finally, draw a different route back to his space shuttle.

Brain stretchers

See if you can solve these puzzles.

Magic number

Follow these steps, writing your answers in the boxes. Try it twice.

	1st go	2nd go
1. Think of a number, then multiply it by 2.	☐	☐
2. Add 12 to the answer.	☐	☐
3. Take away 3 from the answer.	☐	☐
4. Add 5 to the answer.	☐	☐
5. Divide the answer by 2.	☐	☐
6. Take away the original number you thought of. What did you get?	☐	☐

7. Now try again, starting with a different number. What did you get this time?

Bucking broncos

These wild horses need to be put in separate pens. Using a pencil, see if you can make a pen for each horse by drawing just three squares. No curved lines are allowed!

NIGHT SKY

This picture shows the constellation Orion. The stars in the constellation appear to make up the shape of a hunter from Greek mythology. Looking at these views through a telescope, can you spot which one shows Orion?

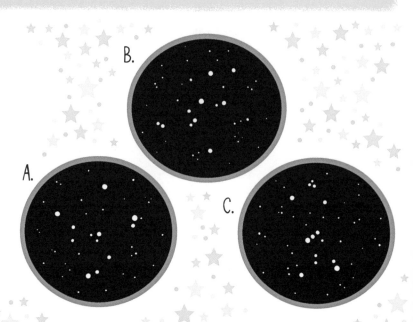

B.

A.

C.

Balancing act

Tightrope walker 3 is about to lose his balance! Each of the juggling balls he is holding weighs a different amount. Draw on the juggling ball or balls that he needs to straighten up.

How many words can you make from the word below? For each new word, you can only use the letters as many times as they appear.

MASTERMIND

WHICH ROBOT?

Look at these robots carefully. Can you see which one matches the black shape?

Up in the air

There are lots of flying machines hidden in the jumble below. How many can you spot?

SPOOKY STUFF

There are lots of haunted mansions in this spooky village. Can you help these boys to reach the safe house? Then, fill in the mansions.

HA HA HA!

Q: What do you do if you see a huge, hairy monster with big pointed teeth?

A: Run!

Which monster in each row is the odd one out? Find it, then fill it in.

GREEN GLOOP

To make some green gloop, you'll need:

half a small glass of cornflour (cornstarch)

quarter of a small glass of cold water

a few drops of green food dye

1. Stir everything in a large bowl.

2. Then, use your hands to mix the gloop.

3. Play with the gloop – try punching it in the bowl, and hold a ball of it in your hand.

ON SAFARI

Spot the animals that you wouldn't expect to see in the African grasslands, then fill them in...

Doodle
markings on
these zebras.

62

SAFARI SEARCH

Can you find the names of four animals that you might see in Africa?

Starting here, draw a line through the letters. You can go up, down, left or right, and the names don't continue on from each other...

```
G O P O Z
I R P B E
L H I R A
L E T N A
A L E P H
```

ANIMAL SUDOKU

Draw pictures of these four animals, to complete the grid on the right:

Every row, every column and every 4-square box in the grid have to include one picture of each animal...

...and each animal can only appear ONCE in each row, column or box.

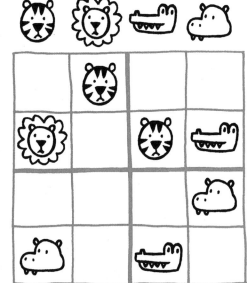

HA HA HA! Q: What do you do if there's a crocodile in your bed?

A: Sleep somewhere else!

SLITHERING SNAKES

Fill in the snakes with an even number of markings with green pens, and the ones with an odd number with orange pens.

DID YOU KNOW?

☆ The biggest land animals in the world are African elephants. Asian elephants are smaller, and have much smaller ears.

☆ No two zebras have exactly the same pattern on their striped coats.

☆ A hunting cheetah can run three times faster than the fastest human being can run.

☆ The hippopotamus gets its name from Greek words meaning 'river horse', because it spends so much time in water.

☆ The giraffe is the tallest animal in the world. A giraffe's tongue can be as long as 50cm (20in).

WHEN IN ANCIENT ROME

PLOT SPOT

It's 44BC and there's a plot to kill the Roman dictator Julius Caesar. Ten of the plotters are trying to hide their daggers in this scene. Can you spot and draw around them all?

HA HA HA!

Q: Who came after the first Roman Emperor?

A: The second one!

CRACK THE CODE

Soldiers in the Roman Army used a code similar to this one. First, find out which letter each letter in the code stands for. Then, translate the message on the right.

A B C D E F G H I
_ _ T _ _ _ X _ Z

J K L M N O P Q R
_ _ _ _ F _ _ _ _

S T U V W X Y Z
J _ _ _ _ _ _ _

RO HXD LAJLT CQRB

LXMN, HXD LXDUM

BNWM BNLANC VNBBJPNB

CX HXDA OARNWMB.

WEAR A TOGA

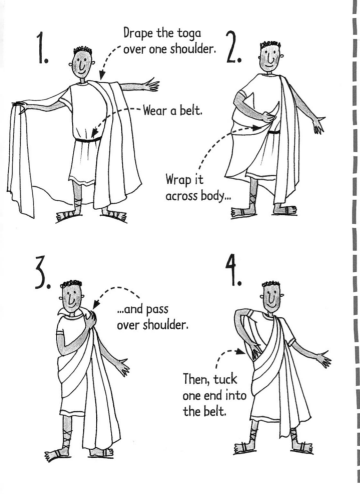

1. Drape the toga over one shoulder.
   Wear a belt.

2. Wrap it across body...

3. ...and pass over shoulder.

4. Then, tuck one end into the belt.

ROMAN NUMBERS

The Romans wrote down numbers using letters of the alphabet:

I = 1   VI = 6   L = 50
II = 2   VII = 7   C = 100
III = 3   VIII = 8   D = 500
IIII* = 4 IX = 9   M = 1000
V = 5   X = 10

When writing longer numbers, they'd write the largest on the left and the smallest on the right, like this:

CXXV= 125 (C + X + X + V = 125)

Now, try filling in these gaps!

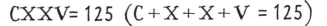

LVI = ... = 133

V + VII = ...   XX - .... = XVII

*Later on, people wrote IV for 4 instead.

ANCIENT EGYPT

Pharaoh's tomb

Deep within a pyramid, an Egyptian pharaoh's tomb has been discovered. Fill the burial chamber with stickers from the sticker pages to show what's been found.

Spells written on the walls in symbols known as hieroglyphs

Sacred scarab beetle – an Egyptian lucky charm

A pharaoh's coffin with a mummy inside*

Baskets of food left for the pharaoh's spirit to eat

Canopic jars containing the mummy's internal organs

*The pharaoh's coffin was often placed in a larger stone coffin called a sarcophagus.

Mummy chase

Draw a line as quickly as you can through the passages and out of the pyramid. Don't go over any of the walls with your pen.

Riddles of the Sphinx

How did a boy fall off a very tall ladder and not get hurt?

What has two heads, four eyes, six legs and a mane?

Which two things can you never have for dinner?

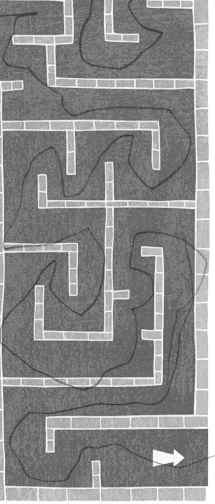

Egyptian code

Crack the code on this Egyptian tablet to find out who's buried nearby.

L I E S   K

A M

W H O

G R E A T   C

FUTURISTIC CITYSCAPE

Add buildings to this
futuristic city.

You could add some
hovering vehicles or
speeding spaceships.

MAD MONSTERS

Use your imagination to complete these monster factcards...

NAME: Slugzilla
EYES: 2 on antennae
LEGS: 0
ICK FACTOR: Its ....
....

NAME: Belcher
EYES: 3
LEGS: 6
ICK FACTOR: Its rotten breath

Read the descriptions and finish drawing the monsters.

NAME: ....
EYES: 5
LEGS: 3
ICK FACTOR: Its greasy fur

NAME: Stickleboy
EYES: ....
LEGS: 2
ICK FACTOR: Its ....

NAME: The Nose
EYES: ....
LEGS: ....
ICK FACTOR: Its spots

NAME: ....
EYES: 4
LEGS: ....
ICK FACTOR:
Its razor sharp teeth

DID YOU KNOW? Some people believe a monster, known as the Yeti, lives in the Himalayan Mountains. Visitors claim to have seen the ape-like creature in the distance and its footprints in the snow.

Hello!

SCRAMBLED WORDS

I'm the Gobble monster. I've been on an eating rampage along a street. Rearrange the letters, to reveal what's in my belly.

kibe ....

reet ....

bchen ....

elepop ....

mapsplot ....

MONSTER SEARCH

C	Y	T	N	I
L	C	O	B	L
O	P	O	I	M
O	S	F	G	E
G	R	E	G	R

Starting in the top left-hand corner, move from square to square, to uncover the names of four monsters. You can move up, down, left or right. Draw a line through the names as you find them.

MARZIPAN MONSTERS

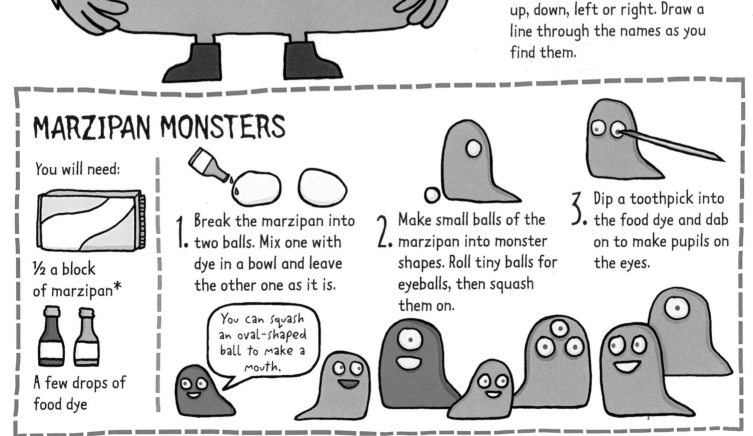

You will need:

½ a block of marzipan*

A few drops of food dye

1. Break the marzipan into two balls. Mix one with dye in a bowl and leave the other one as it is.

2. Make small balls of the marzipan into monster shapes. Roll tiny balls for eyeballs, then squash them on.

3. Dip a toothpick into the food dye and dab on to make pupils on the eyes.

You can squash an oval-shaped ball to make a mouth.

*Marzipan contains nuts, so don't give the monsters to anyone who is allergic to nuts.

Up in the air

Doodle
more planes and
birds in the sky...

Make a whizzer

You'll need:

sticky tape

scissors

2 strips of thin cardboard

2.5cm x 24cm (1 x 9½in)

2.5cm x 12cm (1 x 5in)

4 plastic drinking straws

Cut off this end of each straw.

These pieces should all be the same length.

1. Make loops by overlapping the ends of the strips and pressing on sticky tape.

Tape around the joins, too...

2. Tape two straws inside the bigger loop.

3. Tape the smaller loop inside the straws.

4. Add the other two straws between the first two.

Space them evenly.

Now, hold the whizzer like this...

...and throw it really hard!

It will whizz through the air...

Draw a helicopter...

Draw the cabin, cockpit and tail.

Then, draw the rotor blades and a door.

Add landing skids and other details.

Draw your own helicopter here...

73

LOST IN SPACE

Can you guide the rocket below back to Earth? The correct route passes through nine letters that spell out a space-themed word.

Write the answer here: ....

DRAW AN ALIEN

Draw the head and body.

Add eyes...

...antennae...

...and teeth.

Draw arms and legs too.

Draw your own aliens.

PLANET PUZZLE

The moons orbiting this red planet follow a sequence from the middle outwards. Find out how many should go on the outermost ring by looking at the sequence.

DID YOU KNOW?

☆ The same side of the Moon always faces the Earth.

☆ The Ancient Egyptians thought that the Sun was the god Ra moving across the sky each day in his boat.

☆ Over 300 planets have been discovered outside our Solar System.

☆ The temperature in the middle of the Sun can reach 5 million °C (27 million °F).

☆ Fruit flies were some of the first animals sent into space.

Vanishing tricks

Animals are masters of disguise and use different kinds of camouflage to hide.
They've got lots of tricks... but which of these isn't actually true?

Rocky patch
Stonefish

I hide among rocks in the sea. Don't step on me, as I have deadly poisonous spines.

It's hard for a predator to spot me, as I look just like the trees I live on.

Tree tricks
Leaf-tailed gecko

New coat
Arctic fox

My brownish coat changes to white in the winter, so that I'm hard to see in the snow.

Leaf me alone
Giant leaf insect

I like to sit on leaves, as I look just like one...

The best way for me to avoid hungry birds is to hide on something hairy.

Hairy hide-and-seek
Golden antler moth caterpillar

Sly stripes
Tiger

My stripes blend in with long grasses. I can sneak up on animals that I want to eat.

See how many words you can find hidden in the word

CAMOUFLAGE

Only use each letter the number of times that it appears in the word...

Write your words in this space.

Stealthy shapes

It's not just animals that can hide...
See if you can find these groups of shapes
hidden in the pattern on the right:

Draw around the groups of
shapes when you find them.

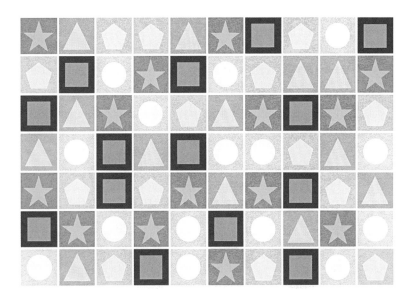

Missing ships

Can you find 15 ships here?

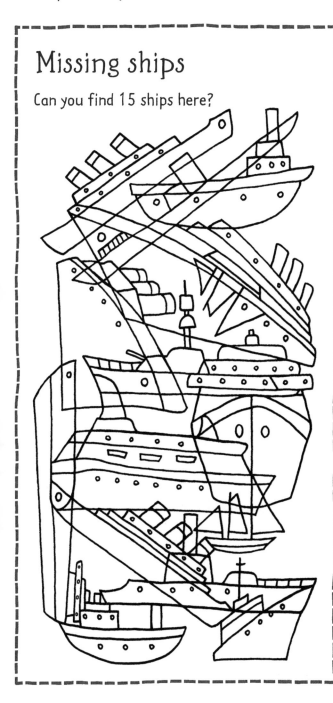

Hidden messages

Below is the same message translated into three
different codes. Draw a line to connect each
coded message with the code that was used:

THE CODES...

(A) Swap the first and last letters of each word.

(B) Write a message, split it into groups of different
numbers of letters, then write each group
backwards, like this: ROBBER – RO B BER – OR B REB

(C) Write the alphabet, then write it backwards
underneath. A becomes Z, B is Y, and so on...

THE MESSAGES...

(1) EM GATE NE CALBT AK XIST.

....

(2) NVVG ZTVMG YOZXP ZG HRC.

....

(3) TEEM TGENA KLACB TA XIS.

....

TIME TRAVEL

You've been given a time machine... but where should you go? Below are some places and times in history you might like to visit, some sights you might see and some dangers to avoid!

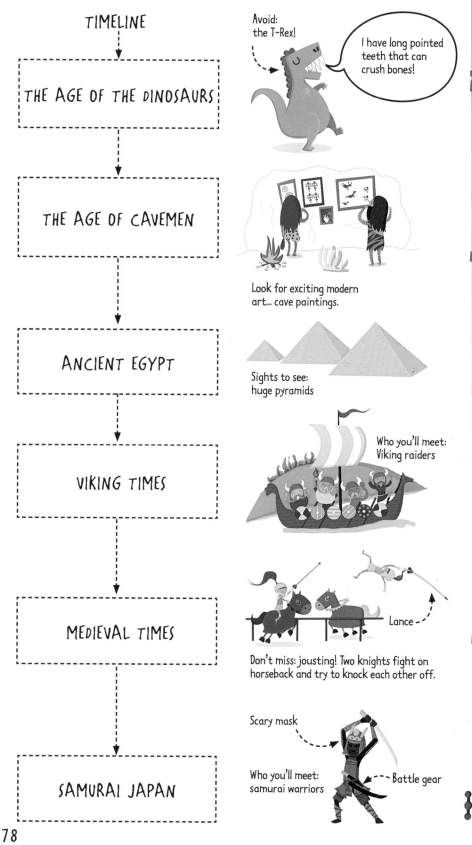

TIMELINE

THE AGE OF THE DINOSAURS

Avoid: the T-Rex!

I have long pointed teeth that can crush bones!

THE AGE OF CAVEMEN

Look for exciting modern art... cave paintings.

ANCIENT EGYPT

Sights to see: huge pyramids

VIKING TIMES

Who you'll meet: Viking raiders

MEDIEVAL TIMES

Lance

Don't miss: jousting! Two knights fight on horseback and try to knock each other off.

SAMURAI JAPAN

Scary mask

Who you'll meet: samurai warriors

Battle gear

Twisted times

These words are in a jumble. Unscramble them and write the correct words in the bottom of the hourglass.

Clue: they're all to do with time.

1. RAYE
2. OCCKL
3. SCONED
4. UNTIME
5. CHAPSWOTT

1. ....
2. ....
3. ....
4. ....
5. ....

HA HA HA!

Q: How do you make time travel?

A: Throw a clock in the air.

A message from the past... or the future

Imagine you've taken a trip through time. Write a note to a friend to tell them about all the exciting things you've seen and the things you've done.

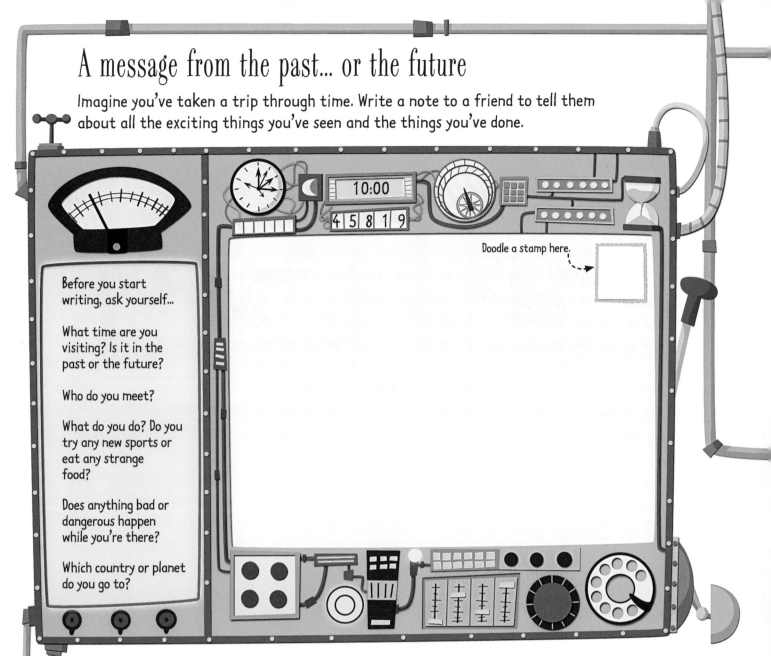

Before you start writing, ask yourself...

What time are you visiting? Is it in the past or the future?

Who do you meet?

What do you do? Do you try any new sports or eat any strange food?

Does anything bad or dangerous happen while you're there?

Which country or planet do you go to?

Doodle a stamp here.

Getting around

It's two hundred years into the future and a new type of vehicle has just been invented. Finish off this doodle to show what it looks like.

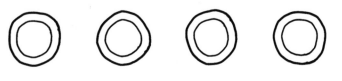

AHOY THERE!

Can you spot 10 differences between these two pirate portraits?

Pirate Quiz

1. Around 300 years ago, thousands of pirates sailed the seas, in the.....................Age of Piracy.
– Was it Silver, Golden or Bronze?

2. Were pirate captains ever in charge of more than one ship?
– Yes or No? ....

3. Is a cutlass...
– A type of rope? A small boat? A short sword? ....

4. What is the name of the flag with a skull and crossbones on it? ....

5. What happened to a pirate who was marooned?
– Was he: Left on an island? Forced to climb the mast? Made to wear a blindfold? ....

Yo ho ho!

Doodle faces on these pirates...

ALL AT SEA...

Fill in this pirate galleon – and draw some pirates on board, if you like.

Fill in five seahorses.

Spot seven similar fish swimming together. Fill them in.

Find seven fish with spots, and fill them in.

DID YOU KNOW?

There are more than 20,000 species of fish in the world. The smallest ones are no bigger than the tip of your finger, and the largest can grow to be longer than buses.

MONSTER TRUCKS

Fill this page with monster trucks
– follow the steps at the bottom
to find out how to draw them.

You could add
patterns and
decorations...

...triangles
for ramps...

...and clouds
of dust.

Draw a monster truck...

Draw the bodywork...

...and two BIG wheels.

Add some windows...

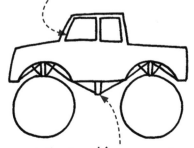

...and the truck's suspension.

Decorate the monster truck...

...and finish off the wheels.

SPORTS PUZZLES

Ball of words

Find these sports words in the ball below. They can go up, down, across and some may even be backwards.

ATHLETICS   FOOTBALL   SKIING
BAT   KARATE   TEAM
CYCLING   PLAYER   VOLLEYBALL

```
        T E B
    A T E Y N U F
  G T K A R A T E D
S K H D M Z L L H C P
C V O L L E Y B A L L
M D E O L V C N G O T A E
B A T Q A I Y P E C X Y O
A J K F B T C Y D L M E B
S C I T E L H T A I R
A H S O P I F W B E L
  R A O G N I I K S
    I F R G E M L
        O L W
```

See how many words you can find in the word

SNOWBOARDER

Only use each letter the number of times that it appears in the word.

Write the words in this space...

League results

	The Lions		The Eagles	
	January to June	July to December	January to June	July to December
Won	4	7	6	5
Lost	5	6	4	6
Drew	8	4	7	6
Points	[ ]	[ ]	[ ]	[ ]
TOTAL POINTS	[ ]		[ ]	

Space for calculations --->

In the league above, each team receives three points for a win, one point for a draw and no points at all if they lose. Looking at these results, which team finishes higher in the league, with more points?

Mixed-up fans

TEN   KEY   FOO   LING

CYC   ETBALL   HOC   TBALL

BASK   NIS

These fans' tops should spell out the names of the sports they support, but they have been mixed up! Link each correct pair of fans back together with a line.

CRAZY SCIENCE LAB

Which funnel does the scientist need to pour the liquid into, to get it into the flask?

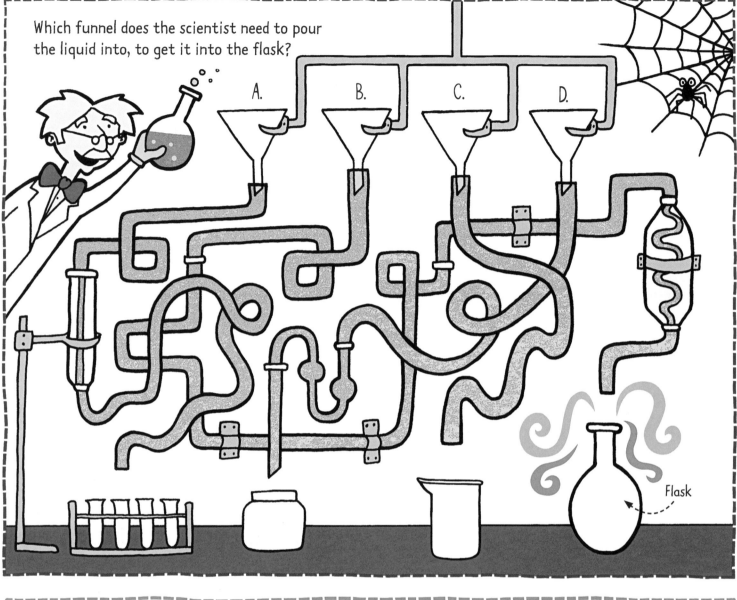

A. B. C. D.

Flask

Bubbling potion

This experiment is exciting. (Don't drink it, though!)

1. Half-fill a jar with vinegar, then add:

several drops of food dye...

...and a good squeeze of dishwashing liquid...

2. Gently stir the mixture, then put the jar on a large tray:

Add a heaped teaspoon of bicarbonate of soda (baking soda)...

3. Stand back and watch the bubbling potion.

Amazing ink

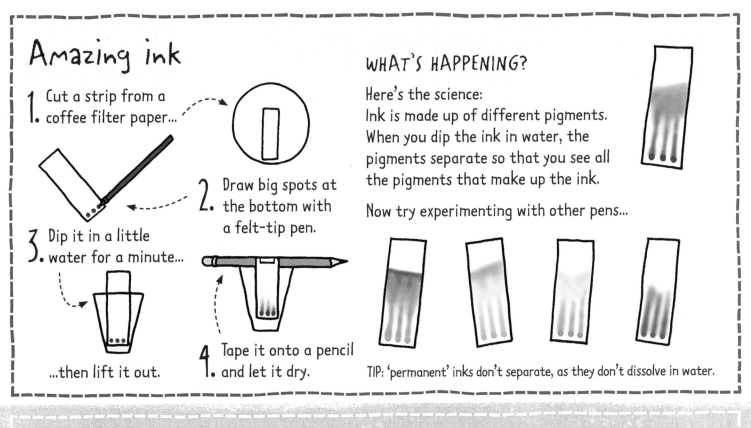

1. Cut a strip from a coffee filter paper...

2. Draw big spots at the bottom with a felt-tip pen.

3. Dip it in a little water for a minute...

...then lift it out.

4. Tape it onto a pencil and let it dry.

WHAT'S HAPPENING?

Here's the science:
Ink is made up of different pigments. When you dip the ink in water, the pigments separate so that you see all the pigments that make up the ink.

Now try experimenting with other pens...

TIP: 'permanent' inks don't separate, as they don't dissolve in water.

Noisy banger

You can make a really LOUD noise using only a piece of paper.

You'll need a large rectangle of newspaper or other thin paper, about 37 x 50cm (15 x 20in).

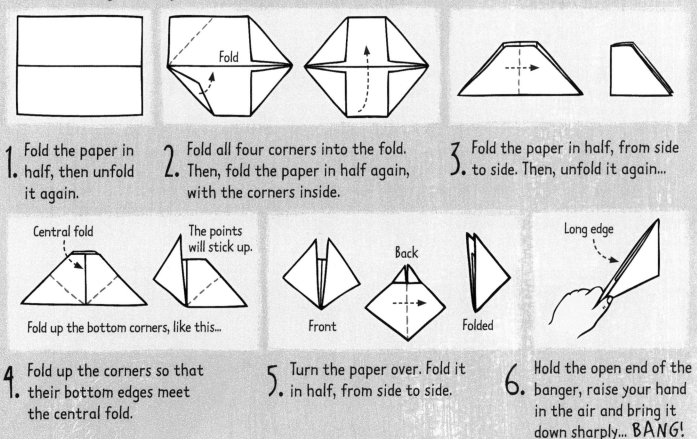

1. Fold the paper in half, then unfold it again.

2. Fold all four corners into the fold. Then, fold the paper in half again, with the corners inside.

3. Fold the paper in half, from side to side. Then, unfold it again...

4. Fold up the corners so that their bottom edges meet the central fold.

5. Turn the paper over. Fold it in half, from side to side.

6. Hold the open end of the banger, raise your hand in the air and bring it down sharply... BANG!

ON THE BATTLEFIELD

The battle has begun! Add stickers from the sticker pages of knights charging on their steeds, soldiers swinging their weapons, and arrows flying through the air.

Weird creatures

Guess that nose

Some creatures have useful, but unusual, noses. Which nose belongs to which creature? Draw lines between the speech bubbles and the correct animals.

A.

> My nose is full of sensors that tell me when food is near.

B.

> I have a big drooping nose that attracts females to me.

C.

> I can blow up my nose to make a loud, honking roar!

D.

> I have 22 'fingers' around my snout that help me to find food.

Elephant seal   Star-nosed mole   Goblin shark   Proboscis monkey

Fact or fiction?

Which of these strange creatures are real and which are imaginary?

Komodo dragons often have blood in their saliva. They attack animals such as goats and swallow them whole.

Griffins live in India. Despite their size, they can fly to great heights. They only use pure gold to build their nests.

A phoenix can live for over 500 years and can only survive in a hot climate. Its cry sounds like a beautiful song.

Vampire squid live in the deepest, darkest part of the ocean. Their long tentacles are covered in sharp spikes.

STAY AWAY!

These animals use tricks to scare away other animals that want to eat them.

Some tarantulas kick itchy hairs from their bodies.

Bombardier beetles fire hot chemicals.

Porcupine fish fill themselves with water to look bigger.

TRUE OR FALSE?

1. A pistol shrimp can snap its claw so hard that it makes powerful bubbles that kill other fish.
   TRUE OR FALSE?

2. A sloth never goes down to the ground.
   TRUE OR FALSE?

3. A rhinoceros beetle can carry 850 times its own body weight.
   TRUE OR FALSE?

4. A basilisk lizard can walk on water.
   TRUE OR FALSE?

5. A kangaroo rat is related to kangaroos.
   TRUE OR FALSE?

Feed the queen

The worker termite in this termites' nest needs to feed the queen. Can you find his way to her chamber?

Termites build their homes out of soil, saliva and droppings.

Worker

Queen

DID YOU KNOW? A queen termite is so big, she can't move. She can be up to 12cm (5in) long.

89

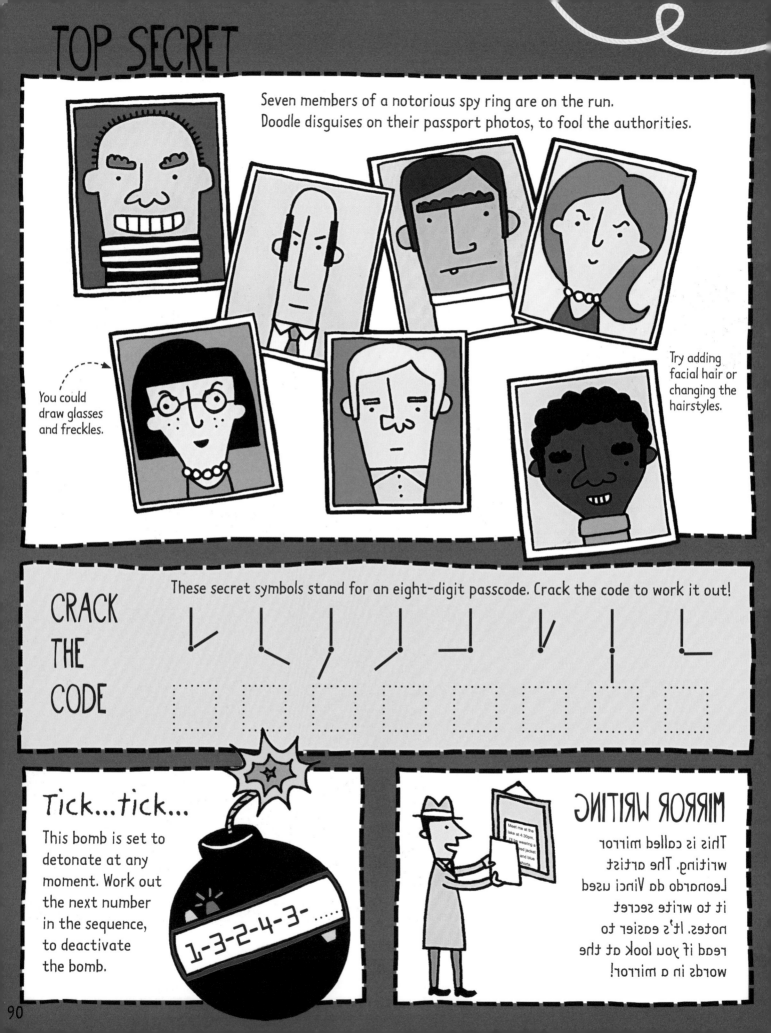

MASTER OF DISGUISE

A good spy needs a good disguise. You can change the way you look with things you find at home.

 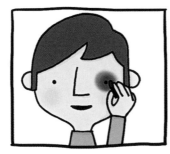

Draw wrinkles around your eyes and lips with a dark eyeliner.

Use blue and black eye shadows, to create bruises or a black eye.

To alter your arms or hands, make some fake cuts.

1. First, paint a line of white glue. When it's almost dry, rub and pinch it a little.

2. Then, draw a wound on the dried gluey 'scab' with a red felt-tip pen.

To disguise your voice on the telephone, try...

...pursing your lips,

...pinching your nose,

...or talking with a big, toothy smile.

Spies used to carry tiny secret messages or microdots. Each message was reduced in size many times until it looked just like an inconspicuous dot.

Spies used to carry tiny secret messages or microdots. Each message was reduced in size many times until it looked just like an inconspicuous dot.

HIDDEN MESSAGES

You can send hidden messages on a piece of newspaper. Just mark dots above the corresponding letters in any newspaper article, in the order they appear.

What message has been hidden on this scrap of newspaper?

LOCKED UP AT LAST

Notorious spy master Bert Le Strange has finally been arrested after eluding inter authorities for ten years.

One of the longest cases in espionage history came to night with the unexpecte awaited arrest of double traitor Bert Le Strange.

Le Strange photographed in one of his many disguises.

Le Strange, 49, was apprehended at the Dutch b passport he presented alerted custom officers t Local police were immediately informed and Le taken into custody. The news of his arrest pro .... across the world,

Answers and solutions

2-3 FAIRGROUND FUN

WHO HIT IT?: Cormac

HIT THE CAN:
The total of the cans is 53.

WORD DARTS:
PRIZES, CARNIVAL, BALLOON, RIDES

LOTS TO SPOT:

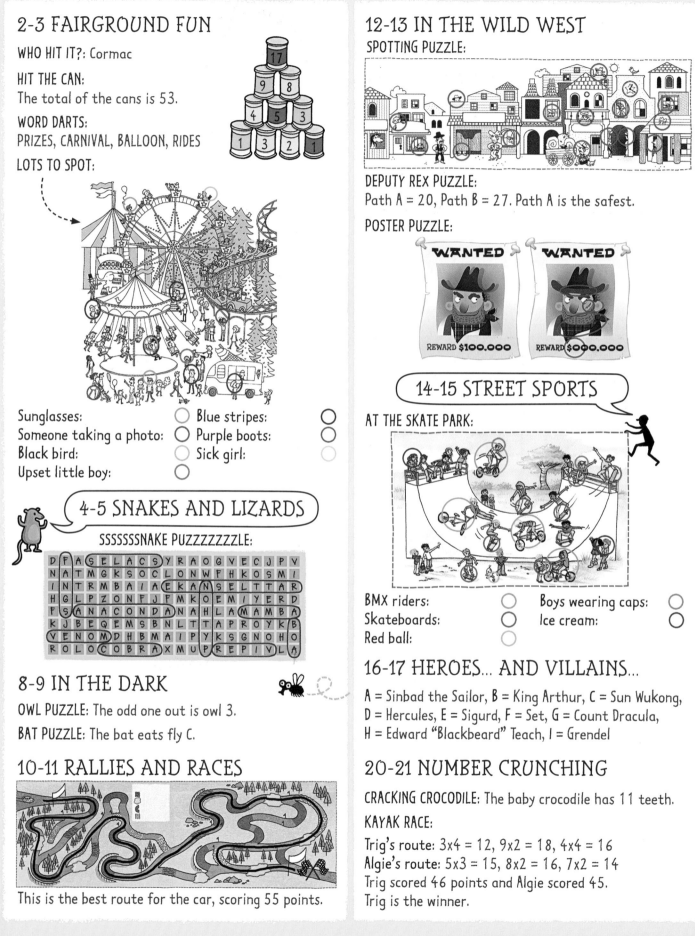

Sunglasses:
Someone taking a photo:
Black bird:
Upset little boy:

Blue stripes:
Purple boots:
Sick girl:

4-5 SNAKES AND LIZARDS

SSSSSSSSNAKE PUZZZZZZZLE:

8-9 IN THE DARK

OWL PUZZLE: The odd one out is owl 3.

BAT PUZZLE: The bat eats fly C.

10-11 RALLIES AND RACES

This is the best route for the car, scoring 55 points.

12-13 IN THE WILD WEST

SPOTTING PUZZLE:

DEPUTY REX PUZZLE:
Path A = 20, Path B = 27. Path A is the safest.

POSTER PUZZLE:

14-15 STREET SPORTS

AT THE SKATE PARK:

BMX riders:
Skateboards:
Red ball:

Boys wearing caps:
Ice cream:

16-17 HEROES... AND VILLAINS...

A = Sinbad the Sailor, B = King Arthur, C = Sun Wukong,
D = Hercules, E = Sigurd, F = Set, G = Count Dracula,
H = Edward "Blackbeard" Teach, I = Grendel

20-21 NUMBER CRUNCHING

CRACKING CROCODILE: The baby crocodile has 11 teeth.

KAYAK RACE:

Trig's route: 3x4 = 12, 9x2 = 18, 4x4 = 16
Algie's route: 5x3 = 15, 8x2 = 16, 7x2 = 14
Trig scored 46 points and Algie scored 45.
Trig is the winner.

KEYPAD CODE: THE CODE NUMBER IS FIFTY SEVEN.

MEET AT NOON -
1x6 2x3 2x3 1x8 1x2 1x8 2x6 3x6 3x6 2x6

ANIMAL NUMBERS:
Snail = 9, Owl = 8, Snake = 2, Flamingo = 4, Penguin = 0

FROM 1 TO 100:

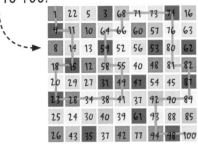

24-25 ROBOTS

BUTTON PUZZLE: The green button will turn on the light.

26-27 JUNGLE ESCAPE

28-29 AT THE MATCH

Rivington Reds' fans: ○   Hotdog mishap: ○
Striped scarves: ○   Not enjoying the game: ○

MATCHING PAIRS:

SPLIT THE BALL:

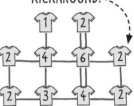

TROPHY TROUBLE:
The odd trophy is 3.

KICKAROUND:

32-33 IN THE SHADOWS

SHAPE UP:
STAR, SQUARE, CIRCLE, HEXAGON, PENTAGON, RECTANGLE

DID YOU KNOW?: Because the sun shines from above at midday, but from the side at sunrise and sunset.

WHICH CAR?: The green car

ODD ONE OUT:
Planet Earth. The others are sources of light.

FAMOUS BUILDINGS:
From left to right: Tower Bridge, Sydney Opera House, Eiffel Tower, Empire State Building

34-35 WHIZZING WHEELS

FIND THE WHEELS...:

SYMMETRY PUZZLE:
Only the steering wheel is symmetrical.

MIXED-UP PLATES: MIRRORS, SPEED, BRAKES, ENGINE, WHEELS

QUICK EXIT: Car 3 was the getaway car.

36-37 BON APPÉTIT

SPAGHETTI PUZZLE:
Chef C cooked the most meatballs.
Chef B didn't make any at all.

PIZZA PUZZLE:
There are two more pepperoni pieces and three fewer mushrooms on each slice of pizza.

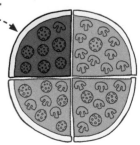

38-39 BURIED TREASURE HUNT

40-41 FLYING HIGH

FLIGHT PLAN:

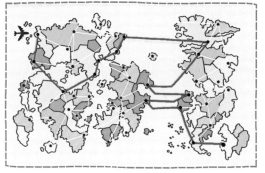

42-43 CREEPY-CRAWLIES

SPIDER QUIZ:
1. Eight, 2. No, 3. True, 4. Tarantulas, 5. True

44-45 EXPLORING EARTH

EXPLORERS PUZZLE:

DUE EAST:

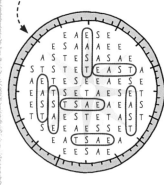

ARCTIC ANIMAL ADVENTURE:

46-47 SPACE STUFF

PLANETS QUIZ:
1. C. Mercury, 2. B. Saturn, 3. B. Jupiter,
4. A. Venus, 5. C. Neptune

WORDSEARCH:

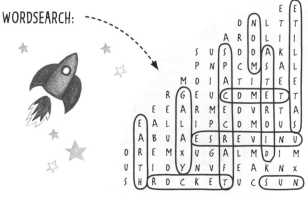

48-49 BIG BATTLE

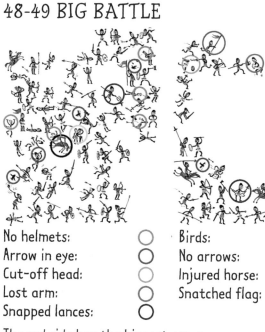

No helmets: ○
Arrow in eye: ○
Cut-off head: ○
Lost arm: ○
Snapped lances: ○

Birds: ○
No arrows: ○
Injured horse: ●
Snatched flag: ○

The red side has the biggest army.
There are 12 soldiers with shields.

50-51 CROOKED CRIMINALS

IDENTITY PARADE: The culprit is E.

SPOT THE DIFFERENCE:

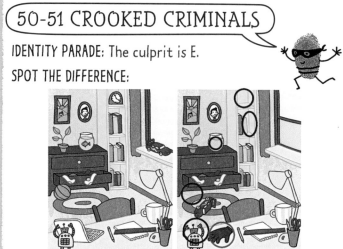

52-53 UNDER THE SEA

54-55 THE GREAT OUTDOORS

BUG SEARCH:

FOREST MAZE:

LEAVING MESSAGES:

ALL IN A TANGLE:
The climber wearing green gets to the top of the mountain.

58-59 BRAIN STRETCHERS

BUCKING BRONCOS:

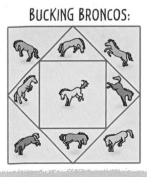

NIGHT SKY: C.

WHICH ROBOT?:

BALANCING ACT:
Draw a striped ball in his right hand.

UP IN THE AIR: 7

60-61 SPOOKY STUFF

HAUNTED MAZE:

ODD ONE OUT:

62-63 ON SAFARI

SLITHERING SNAKES:

SAFARI SEARCH:

Gorilla
Hippo
Elephant
Zebra

```
G   O   P   O   Z
    R   P   B   E
L   H   I   R   A
L   E   T   N   A
A   E   L   E   P   H
```

ANIMAL SUDOKU:

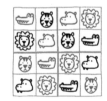

64-65 WHEN IN ANCIENT ROME

PLOT SPOT:

CRACK THE CODE:
If you crack this code, you could send secret messages to your friends.

ROMAN NUMBERS:
LVI = 56, CXXXIII = 133,
V + VII = XII, XX - III = XVII

66-67 ANCIENT EGYPT

RIDDLES OF THE SPHINX:
1. He fell off the lowest step. 2. A man on a horse
3. Breakfast and lunch

EGYPTIAN CODE:
HERE LIES KING RAMESES
HE WHO READS THIS WILL FIND GREAT RICHES

70-71 MAD MONSTERS

SCRAMBLED WORDS:
kibe = bike, reet = tree,
bchen = bench,
elepop = people,
mapsplot = lamppost

MONSTER SEARCH:
Cyclops
Ogre
Bigfoot
Gremlin

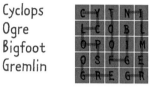

74-75 LOST IN SPACE

SPACE MAZE:

PLANET PUZZLE:

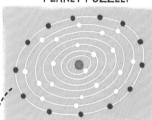

13 moons - the sum of the moons on the two previous rings

The word is ASTRONAUT.

76-77 VANISHING TRICKS

ANIMAL PUZZLE:

All the tricks are true apart from the one about the golden antler moth caterpillar.

HIDDEN MESSAGES:
1. CODE B
2. CODE C
3. CODE A

STEALTHY SHAPES:

78-79 TIME TRAVEL

TWISTED TIMES:
1. YEAR, 2. CLOCK, 3. SECOND,
4. MINUTE, 5. STOPWATCH

80-81 AHOY THERE!

SPOT THE DIFFERENCE:

PIRATE QUIZ:
1. Golden, 2. Yes, 3. A short sword,
4. The Jolly Roger, 5. Left on an island

82-83 SPORTS PUZZLES

BALL OF WORDS:

LEAGUE RESULTS:
The Eagles finish higher with 46 points. The Lions finish with 45 points.

MIXED-UP FANS:
TEN-NIS, FOO-TBALL,
CYC-LING, HOC-KEY,
BASK-ETBALL

84-85 CRAZY SCIENCE LAB

FUNNEL PUZZLE: B.

88-89 WEIRD CREATURES

GUESS THAT NOSE:
A. Goblin shark
B. Proboscis monkey
C. Elephant seal
D. Star-nosed mole

TRUE OR FALSE?:
1. T, 2. F, 3. T,
4. T, 5. F

FACT OR FICTION?:
Only komodo dragons and vampire squid are real.

FEED THE QUEEN:

90-91 TOP SECRET

CRACK THE CODE: 2 4 7 8 9 1 6 3

TICK... TICK...: 1 - 3 - 2 - 4 - 3 - 5
(Sequence: +2, -1, +2, -1, +2)

HIDDEN MESSAGES:
The password is tortoise.

Additional illustrations by Paul Nicholls

This edition first published in 2014 by Usborne Publishing Ltd., Usborne House, 83-85 Saffron Hill, London EC1N 8RT, England. www.usborne.com © 2014, 2011 Usborne Publishing Ltd. The name Usborne and the devices 🔔 are Trade Marks of Usborne Publishing Ltd. All rights reserved. No part of this publication may be reproduced, stored in a retrieval system or transmitted in any form or by any means, electronic, mechanical, photocopying, recording or otherwise without the prior permission of the publisher. UE. First published in America in 2012.